SHW

ALLEN COUNTY PUBLIC LIBRARY

3 1833 02321 3439

P9-BIO-370

947 R44f   MAR 3 1 1994
Riff, M. A.
The face of survival

DO NOT REMOVE
CARDS FROM POCKET

ALLEN COUNTY PUBLIC LIBRARY
FORT WAYNE, INDIANA 46802

You may return this book to any agency, branch,
or bookmobile of the Allen County Public Library.

DEMCO

The Face of Survival

Jewish Life in Eastern Europe
Past and Present

Michael Riff

With personal memoirs by
Hugo Gryn, Stephen Roth, Ben Helfgott
and Hermy Jankel

Epilogue by Rabbi Moses Rosen

VALLENTINE MITCHELL

Allen County Public Library
900 Webster Street
PO Box 2270
Fort Wayne, IN 46801-2270

First published 1992 in Great Britain by Vallentine Mitchell & Co. Ltd,
Gainsborough House, Gainsborough Road, London, E11 1RS, England

Copyright © 1992 Vallentine Mitchell & Co. Ltd

British Library Cataloguing in Publication Data
Riff, M.A. (Michael A.)
  The face of survival: Jewish life in Eastern Europe past and present.
  1. Eastern Europe. Jews. Social life, history
  I. Title
  947.0004924

  ISBN 0-85303-220-3

*All rights reserved. No part of this publication may be reproduced in any form
or by any means, electronic, mechanical, photo-copying, recording or otherwise,
without the prior permission of Vallentine Mitchell & Co. Limited.*

Designed by Zena Flax
Typeset by Print Origination, Hants
Printed in Great Britain by BPCC Wheatons Ltd, Exeter

Contents

Prologue

The fall of communism has initiated an unparalleled period of change in Eastern Europe. In Czechoslovakia, Hungary, Poland and Romania political life, the economies and social order are in a state of much-welcomed transformation. Hope for the future is transcending the gloom and pessimism of the present.

There exists a bitter-sweet view of these developments for many Eastern European Jews and their descendants. Our fate was intimately intertwined with the history of Eastern Europe. Much of what we are today is a result of what happened in this world. For over a thousand years, the form and content of our existence as Jews was to a great extent shaped in the cities, towns and villages of Poland, Hungary, Romania and Czechoslovakia.

For all but a handful, this world came to an abrupt and violent end as a consequence of Hitler's war against the Jews. As a new political order unfolds, life will improve. But Eastern European Jewry will never be anything but a glimmer of what it was.

While we mourn and remember the physical destruction of the lives and civilization of our people, we should recognize that Jewish life has not been extinguished in Eastern Europe. Despite continuing persecution, demoralization, intermarriage and emigration, numbers of Jewish men, women and children continue to live as Jews in the region. The survival of these communities is as much a testimony to the tenacity and courage of individuals as to the strength of Jewish cohesiveness.

What the future will hold for the Jews in Eastern Europe is not clear. Recent experience has shown that to one degree or another outpourings of anti-Semitism have accompanied the political and socio-economic dislocation following the demise of communism. As disturbing as its extent has been the familiarity of its content. Even though small in number, the Jews in Eastern Europe have often become scapegoats and objects of hate. Once again, we are forced to realize the depths of anti-Jewish prejudice in the area.

At the same time, the coming of democratic institutions and values has assisted the renewal of Jewish communal institutions and the restoration of free contact with Israel. University programs in Jewish studies are being established, conferences are held on subjects of Jewish interest and a multitude of publications on Jewish subjects are appearing in the bookstores.

Equally significant, political and church leaders have spoken out against anti-Semitism and have identified their efforts to counteract it as part of the general struggle for democracy and toleration. Unlike before the Second World War, there is a general realization that even the toleration of anti-Semitism can be detrimental to improved economic and political ties with the United States and Western Europe.

Through its words and pictures, *Face of Survival* tells the story of East European Jewry since the turn of the century. It illuminates the past and helps us interpret the present. Revealed are the vitality and fortitude of a people determined to survive.

Abraham J. Foxman
National Director
Anti-Defamation League

Acknowledgements

We are grateful to Eva Mitchell, former Director of the Central British Fund, and to the C.B.F. for their co-operation in producing this publication and for the important and valuable material and information they have provided from their own existing resources. Their continuing involvement and support on behalf of Jewish communities portrayed in this book are a major contribution to a better quality of life in the countries concerned.

The Jewish community organisations and institutions in Poland, Czechoslovakia, Hungary and Romania gave invaluable assistance with itinerary and hospitality during our visits.

We express our deep gratitude to Frank Cass for his patience, counsel and advice throughout our visits, research, planning and execution of this project and not least for his initial encouragement and interest when we first embarked upon the original idea for the book.

We thank Michael Freedland for all his efforts in much of the original drafting of the text, extensive interviewing of certain of the contributors and for the research, collation and editing of a large number of the photographs that appear. Thanks are also due to Patricia Mandel, who completed the selection of illustrations (and who sadly died before the book went into production). The persons and institutes listed in the photo and map credits are thanked for permission to reproduce the photographs and maps in the book. The inclusion of some of the photographs has been justified by their historical interest rather than their technical quality.

The advice and assistance of the Institute of Jewish Affairs, the World Jewish Congress, Professor Antony Polonsky, Jonathan Freedland and Roman Halter are also acknowledged.

PL and IW

Foreword

Any visit to Israel must mean a pilgrimage to Yad Vashem to keep the commandment: 'Remember what Amalek did to you when you left Egypt'. We felt that to remember properly what that modern Amalek, Hitler, had done to our people it was necessary to visit the communities he had succeeded in destroying. Our objective, then, was to achieve for ourselves a greater understanding of our roots in Eastern Europe and the magnificence of that Jewish culture which had flourished there for centuries. Little did we know then how moved we would be by what we were to see and how, amidst the pain of remembering the suffering and the destruction of not only the millions of precious lives but of the culture which had taken generations to develop, there would be glimmers of hope as we witnessed the valiant efforts of those remaining to keep their heritage alive and to rebuild Jewish life in a spiritual wasteland.

In our journeys we were fortunate to have with us individuals who had themselves experienced the ravages of the Holocaust, to guide us through the countries which had rejected them. Hugo Gryn, Ben Helfgott and Stephen Roth shared with us their memories and gave meaning to every path we travelled. With them we found 'sermons in stones'. These personal accounts, together with a fourth from Hermy Jankel, form the central section of the book.

We are also grateful to Rabbi Moses Rosen who explained to us the creative tension of Jewish life in Romania. There we saw the Jewish schools which had been built out of the ashes; the intensity of Jewish learning and identification of large numbers of children who, like their ancestors' generations, had been taught to dream of returning to their homeland, Eretz Yisroel, but who, unlike them, could now realise this dream because of the leadership of this great Rabbi.

We visited Poland, Czechoslovakia, Hungary and Romania. In each community we were received with great excitement, which was expressed by an endearing openness and generous hospitality. Much is written and spoken of the remnants of Jewish life in Eastern Europe but little or nothing exists to portray the continuing perseverance and courage of those who remain and who continue to maintain a truly Jewish life in these countries. We therefore decided to publish our experiences in this photographic essay and we hope that this book will create a greater awareness of the continued existence of such communities among Western Jews whose lives have not been influenced by such dark events, who have been able to flourish and who have been accepted in free and democratic societies. Historic political changes have occurred in Eastern Europe since our visits took place and since 1990 life has become somewhat more tolerable for the Jewish communities and travel in both directions less restricted. However, the extreme national feelings currently being experienced everywhere may make Jews more vulnerable to antisemitism and the consequences that can flow from this.

We dedicate this book not only to the victims of the Holocaust but also to those who have survived and are perpetuating Jewish life in Eastern Europe. Our love and concern for these communities of the past and present will, we hope, be conveyed to all who read this book, and inspire them also to make similar pilgrimages and thus give courage to those remnants of our people who stand to give testimony that in the end Hitler did not win.

Peter L Levy
Israel Weinstock

Jewish Life
in Eastern Europe –
the Past

Europe at the outbreak of the First World War

Antony Polonsky: The Little Dictators *(Routledge & Kegan Paul)*

Introduction

Only the most pessimistic observer could foresee, even as late as 1939 or 1940, the full extent of the tragedy that was about to befall European Jewry. Yet, the years immediately preceding World War Two were for the Jews of East Central Europe portentous with disaster. The hope that the 1914–18 war had been the war to end all wars was already a meaningless fiction. Mussolini and Hitler had for all intents and purposes broken the peace and Europe seemed on the edge of open conflict. Moreover, in all the countries of the region, with the notable exception of Czechoslovakia, in both legal and economic terms the situation of the Jews was becoming increasingly precarious. Laws and regulations, including the infamous *numerus clausus* which limited the number of Jewish young people able to attend secondary schools and universities, were introduced relegating the Jews to the position of second-class citizens in Poland and Romania as well as Hungary.

Especially in Poland, moreover, restrictions on their participation in the economy exacerbated an already bad situation brought on by the depression, so that by the late 1930s one in three Jewish families was dependent on the receipt of welfare payments from the American Jewish Joint Distribution Committee (known as 'The Joint') and other Jewish relief organizations. The 'Jewish problem' was no longer seen in terms of achieving legal equality or assimilation, but became a matter of physical survival.

In Poland, moreover, and quite some time before the Nazi invasion, only mass emigration held the prospect of a solution to the plight of the Jews. It was, of course, sadly a time when immigration restrictions in both Palestine and the United States made it difficult, if not impossible, for Jews anywhere to find a place of refuge. As the memoirs of Stephen Roth bear out, the situation in Hungary, even though not as bleak as in Poland or Romania, was far from hopeful. Antisemitism had grudgingly to be accepted as a fact of life. Gone were the halcyon days of the Dual Monarchy when the Jews, rightfully for the most part, considered themselves as an integral constituent of the ruling Magyar element in the Hungarian half of the Habsburg Empire.

Before the First World War

The story of how this situation came to be starts in the period before the First World War when the lands which constituted the states of Poland, Czechoslovakia, Hungary and Romania were, with the exception of most of the latter, still part of either the Austro-Hungarian, German or Russian Empires. One could perhaps argue that any meaningful history of the Jews of these territories should really begin much earlier, in the seventeenth century, when the country with the most extensive domains and largest Jewish population was the Kingdom of Poland. For it was the demographic re-configuration of the region's Jewish population following its decline and eventual demise over the next 250 years which constitutes, in a sense, an unspoken sub-text of our story. In other words, it was on account of the migration of Jews westward and southward from the Polish lands ever since about 1650 that much of what was to become Romania, Hungary, Czechoslovakia obtained sizeable Jewish populations in the first place. Such territories as Northeastern Slovakia, Sub-Carpathian Ruthenia and Transylvania were, thus, almost exclusively inhabited by the descendants of Jews who had come from neighbouring Poland. This was a development not just of the late nineteenth or twentieth centuries but of the entire period since the second half of the seventeenth century. There were of course periods when the pace of migration quickened. These were times of crisis, as for example after the Chmielnicki Revolt of 1648, or in the second half of the eighteenth century when Poland's political decline made migration a virtual necessity.

For the regions to which Polish Jews migrated there were consequences for both their external and internal development. The most noticeable impact was obviously felt in sheer demographic terms. Concentrations of Jewish population arose in, for example, Sub-Carpathian Ruthenia or Transylvania akin to those in neighbouring Galicia. In conjunction with the similarly underdeveloped economic conditions of these areas it made for a replication of Polish Jewry's social structure. Families were large, in which it was not all that uncommon for men to devote their time almost exclusively to study and prayer, while the women – often literally – minded the store. Jewish publicans, shopkeepers, produce merchants and, later on, industrialists played a conspicuously disproportionate role in the local economies and, as a consequence, constituted *de facto* together with non-Jewish teachers and officials the local middle class. At the same time, to one degree or another and depending on the area, many Jews led marginal existences as petty traders or even day labourers and farmers. This was particularly so in Sub-Carpathian Ruthenia, which in the pre-war period had the highest per capita Jewish population in Europe.

As in other such areas, even though by the 1930s the Zionists and the Left had made significant inroads amongst the labouring poor and educated youths of the towns, religious life remained firmly in the hands of the Orthodox and Chassidim. Not unexpectedly, as in neighbouring Poland too, the overwhelming majority of Jews spoke Yiddish, even if they were also often fluent in Hungarian which had been the language of the Jewish elite since the late nineteenth century. Amongst this group the knowledge of German was not uncommon. It had a certain snob appeal, of course, but it was also a kind of *lingua franca* amongst the Jews as well as the business community of East Central Europe. Since most Jews were engaged in one form of commerce or another, often as intermediaries in a rural setting, they also knew at least enough of the local Ukrainian dialect to converse with their customers. In independent Czechoslovakia, a fair number of the younger generation learned Czech through attendance at secular state schools intended originally for the children of officials and business people from Bohemia and Moravia working in the region. Significantly, such schools were regarded by the dominant Chassidic and Orthodox majority as preferable to the avowedly Zionist Hebrew High Schools set up in Munkačevo and Užhorod along the lines of the *Tarbut* schools in Poland, where they were also boycotted by the traditional majority. In any case, as Hugo Gryn's rather rueful comments amusingly indicate, it was not at all uncommon in Jewish families for more than one or even two languages to be spoken in the home with equal ease.

Poland

With some variation, the above situation prevailed in large parts of Poland, especially Galicia, which like Sub-Carpathian Ruthenia and Transylvania had formerly been part of the Austro-Hungarian monarchy. In Galicia, as the Polish territories of the Habsburgs were called, after the duchy of the same name located in the western part of the province, from the 1880s onwards considerable change in external political and economic conditions took place. Earlier, of course, the Jewish Enlightenment, or *Haskalah*, also brought a measure of change within the Jewish community. The *Maskilim*, as the propagators of the *Haskalah* were called, endeavoured not only to introduce religious reforms and revive Hebrew letters but also, as in Germany before, advocated the cause of modernization, acculturation and integration. The inevitable consequence was a measure of linguistic/cultural, political and socio-economic re-alignment amongst the Jews of the province. As the Poles gained greater political power and cultural autonomy an increasing number of younger Jews, almost exclusively the sons and daughters of the urban middle and upper middle classes, sought, and sometimes attained, varying forms of cultural and political integration with the Polish majority. They became by their own definition 'Poles of the Mosaic Faith'. This was not, it has to be emphasized, a phenomenon of the *shtetl* or village of economically backward eastern Galicia where Yiddish, Orthodoxy and Chassidism reigned supreme and the majority of the province's Jews lived. It had the effect, as well, of inevitably drawing the Jews into the developing national conflict between the Poles and the Ukrainian majority of the East. Economic development, however limited in scope, necessarily brought Jews into the ranks of the bourgeoisie and the working classes. This situation encouraged amongst the younger acculturated Jews the rise not only of socialism but also of Jewish nationalism. The former gave rise to a state of affairs whereby on the eve of war in 1914 there was considerable Jewish participation in Social Democracy as well as a viable, if much weaker Yiddish-oriented Jewish socialism than in Russian Poland. Similarly, amongst the Jewish nationalists there were both a powerful Zionist movement and the politically important autonomists, who actually held seats in the local as well as imperial parliaments and had achieved practical gains, most notably in the educational and cultural field.

So it came to pass that in Galicia a situation developed whereby in certain areas and amongst certain sections of the Jewish population conditions approximating those in the western and more economically developed provinces of Bohemia or Moravia began to emerge. The difference, and ultimately the problem too, was that this transformation was really quite limited in scope. Conditions in the east of 'Austrian Poland', except in cities such as Lwów (Lemberg) and Brody, remained virtually intact until 1914. Even in western Galicia, moreover, nothing like the economic development of the Bohemian Crownlands which could have given birth to a numerous and independent bourgeoisie took place.

Economic and political changes also affected the situation in those areas of Poland under Tsarist domination. This was especially the case in the so-called Congress Kingdom, the autonomy of which had been granted by the Congress of Vienna but was virtually abolished after 1863. Although admittedly starting from a low base, in the decade between 1860 and 1870 industrial production increased almost three-fold. The capital, Warsaw, became a truly large and industrial city with a population of 650,000 of whom almost a third were Jews. Lódz grew to be a major textile centre with a population of 350,000. In this development as elsewhere in Central Europe, Jewish industrialists and financiers played a prominent part. A type of Jewish commercial and industrial bourgeoisie emerged in both cities which really had no direct equivalent in Austrian Poland. Where they did have a good deal in common was in the behaviour of their offspring, many of whom became 'Poles of the Mosaic persuasion', even if the political and economic incentives present in Galicia were entirely lacking in the Congress Kingdom.

From the 1880s onwards, however, economic difficulties in the agricultural sector brought about by Russian confiscations and, as elsewhere, by increasing competition from North American and other overseas producers and Russia disturbed this situation. Ever larger numbers of Poles moved to the towns, where they found the Jew not in his traditional role as an intermediary in the rural economy but as a real or perceived competitor. The situation was exacerbated by Russian policies discriminating against the employment of Poles in the Civil Service, but the basic fact remained that Jews, not only as entrepreneurs and financiers but as doctors and shopkeepers, effectively constituted the urban bourgeoisie of the Congress Kingdom. Although tension between the two groups grew, increasing antisemitism was not an immediate consequence. The Polish leadership at the time favoured the integration of the Jews into the Polish community which had already begun, as we have seen, in the form of increasing acculturation amongst the Jewish middle classes of the cities.

By the 1890s the relative state of harmony between Jews and Poles in the Congress Kingdom began to break down. The growing conflict between the Jewish and Polish middle classes in the cities combined with increasing nationalism amongst the Poles, intensified by the Tsarist programme of russification, to make the situation ripe for political antisemitism. Aggravated by the influx of Jews from Lithuania and Byelorussia in search of greater freedom and better economic opportunities, it found its expression in the National Democratic Party led by Roman Dmowski, who remained at its helm until well after the formation of independent Poland. Convinced that only a small percentage of Jews could be 'absorbed' by the Polish nation, the rest who, in his view, impeded the formation of a native Polish middle class should be forced to emigrate.

Within about a decade Dmowski's views no longer seemed as radical as when they were first put forward. Even among former Liberals and former positivists a kind of 'progressive antisemitism' took hold which called for a 'de-judaising' of the towns and rejected the notion that Jews could be integrated into the Polish community. The culmination of these developments came in 1912 after the elections to the fourth Russian Duma (parliament) in which the Jewish voters of Warsaw by lending their support to the Socialist as the only non-antisemitic candidate helped him to victory in a three-way race. Dmowski who had stood for the National Democrats and his followers decided to retaliate by organizing a boycott of Jewish-owned shops throughout Congress Poland.

While in Warsaw and Lódz there was little or no physical abuse of Jews, in the countryside the situation took a more violent turn. The worst incident was in the town of Planów, southwest of Lódz, where in May 1913 a mob burnt down a Jewish shop and killed seven Jews. Clearly, the Jews of the Congress Kingdom now had to contend with not only a Polish leadership that was with few exceptions avowedly antisemitic, but also a population whose hostility could easily be transformed into physical violence.

Although remaining outwardly calm, there were some disquieting signs in the relationship between Jews and Poles in Galicia as well. Elements within the nascent peasants' movement in the western part of the province had adopted as part of their programme a plank calling for an end to domination by Jews of petty trade, which had become commonplace earlier in Germany and the Bohemian Crownlands. In Lwów, where the Poles increasingly saw themselves in an embattled situation *vis-à-vis* the Ukrainian majority of the surrounding countryside, groups aligned with the National Democrats attracted increased support. On the whole, however, in Austrian Poland the aristocratic conservatives who had ruled the province since the granting of autonomy in the 1860s successfully opposed the adoption of the antisemitic policies of their populist-inclined opponents.

Two regions of what became Poland after 1918 not mentioned till now, Prussian Poland (Posen, Pomerania and Upper Silesia) and the so-called *Kresy* (Polish Lithuania-Byelorussia and Volynia)

A goose-seller in one of the
Jewish markets of Warsaw,
1899. Goose dishes were
favourites on the tables of those
Jews who could afford it, usually
on the Sabbath and feast days.
California Museum of Photography,
Keystone-Mast Collection
University of California, Riverside

A huge proportion of Warsaw's
population was Jewish. Market
day in any one of its Jewish
districts gives an idea of how
strong that Jewish influence was.
The Hulton Picture Company

An elderly Jewish 'man of the road' with his grandson. The road is from Warsaw to Otwock, one of the rural towns surrounding the capital.
Yivo Institute, New York

Klezmorim – traditional musicians, most of whom are members of the Faust family of Rohatyn, in 1912.
Yivo Institute, New York

Jewish labourer in a Polish
timber yard.
The Hulton Picture Company

The executive committee of the
Bakery Workers' Union in
Czestochowa, Poland,
1912–1917.
*Bund Archive of the Jewish Labour
Movement*

The young Jews pictured here,
members of a Zionist youth group
in Wysokie Mazowieckie in
1917, left for Palestine in 1920.
Sonia Kolodny, Israel

Breakfast in the girls' Jewish
elementary school at Wysokie
Mazowieckie, 1918.
Sonia Kolodny, Israel

A Jewish apple-seller at Wysokie
Mazowieckie, near Bialistok, one
of the main centres of Jewish
urban settlement – early 1920s.
Sonia Kolodny, Israel

An all-too familiar sight – the
results of a pogrom. At
Proskaura, February 1919.
The Hulton Picture Company

A demonstration in London, June
1919, protesting against pogroms
in Poland.
The Hulton Picture Company

A Jew whose beard has been cut off by Polish soldiers in Lódz 1923.
Yivo Institute, New York

Boys cheder, Lublin, 1924.
Yivo Institute, New York

The Warsaw Jewish Theatre still flourishes in the Polish capital – with a number of its performers who are not Jewish. No such need in the 1920s when this group performed in Wysokie Mazowieckie.
Sonia Kolodny, Israel

Enjoying the Planty gardens in Cracow in the 1920s.
Polish Government archive

The pre-war Polish synagogue
choirs – like this one at the
Grodzisk Mazowieckie synagogue
near Warsaw in 1930 – set a
pattern that was copied
throughout Britain and America.
Haia Warina, Tel Aviv

On the river at the popular Jewish resort of Szczannica in 1932.
Polish Government archive

A Zionist youth brass band in Bedzin, April 1935.
Tel Itzhak, Masoah Archive

**Part of the wall of the Warsaw
Ghetto.**
Mandel Archive

which were under the Russian Empire, remained, if for very different reasons, almost completely free of the type of antisemitic agitation which took place in Congress Poland or to a much lesser degree in Galicia. In the former the 'Jewish problem' had solved itself by demographic change. There were only 20,000 Jews left in the region, the majority having migrated to Berlin and Breslau. Those Jews remaining, moreover, had become acculturated to the German minority. Even though the Polish political scene was dominated by the National Democrats, the issue of antisemitism was avoided since it would have alienated the progressive element amongst the Germans to whom the Poles looked for support. Polish nationalists, moreover, looked upon the situation in the area with the vast majority of the Jews having 'emigrated' as a model of what might happen in the rest of Poland.

The situation could not have been more different in the *Kresy*. It was an area characterized by ethnic diversity and economic as well as political backwardness. Although historically ruled by the Polish nobility, except in the cities and amongst the landowners the Polish element was weak. Economic backwardness helped preserve the *shtetl* as a viable institution and meant the larger towns had sizeable, if not majority Jewish populations. Coupled with the ethnic diversity it helped explain the relative absence of antisemitism in the region. Even the pogroms of the Tsarist period hardly affected the Lithuanian-Byelorussian lands and the Polish nationalists failed to make any serious inroads. If Jews acculturated, it was not towards the Poles but the Russians, who after all exercised hegemony over the area. But relatively few actually did, since even in the towns there were more Jews than Russians. There were also other reasons why an assimilationist tendency such as in Congress Poland or Galicia was almost entirely lacking in especially the Lithuanian-Byelorussian lands. Chassidism had traditionally been relatively weak there, which allowed the Jewish Enlightenment or *Haskalah* to strike unusually deep roots with unparalleled strength.

Characterized by its emphasis on Hebrew language and culture, it nurtured the rise of modern Jewish politics. The Jewish socialist party known as the *Bund* was founded there in 1897 as was the religious Zionist or Mizrachi movement some years later. Zionism generally had a strong popular base there from the very beginning. Even if russified, the Jewish intellectuals of Lithuania-Byelorussia were much more likely than those almost anywhere else in Europe to join Jewish political movements.

Clearly, the experience of the Jews in Poland was marked by a high degree of diversity reflecting the history and conditions prevailing in each of the hegemonies in which they lived. In end effect then, the Jews of Poland did not comprise one Jewry but several, each of which was in turn divided into a number of groups and sub-groups. As we shall see, this situation could not help but influence the shape of things to come, both in terms of the internal development of the Jewish minority and its relations to the Polish state and society. Yet, as we shall also see, with the passage of time Polish Jewry, in a sense, re-constituted itself. It was not as if the differences between the various types of Jews who lived in Poland disappeared or that the past did not generally weigh heavily on the reality of Jewish life between the wars but that Jewish communal behaviour came increasingly under the influence of the present rather than the past. To put it in a slightly different way, the changing circumstances of interwar Poland made for a new reality in which the Jewish experience too underwent transformation.

Czechoslovakia
(Bohemia, Moravia, Slovakia and
Sub-Carpathian Ruthenia)

Before looking at the all-important period of the First World War and its immediate aftermath, let us turn to the other societies under consideration. If Poland and Romania were the two countries where Jews fared worst in the interwar period, it was in Czechoslovakia that conditions were best. This was no accident and had much to do with the experience of the lands comprising the Czechoslovak Republic before independence. As indicated earlier, Czechoslovak Jewry despite its common, as it were, 'Habsburg ancestry', was not a single unit, but rather an agglomeration of several different Jewries. Partly, as in Poland, the differences were accounted for by previous hegemony: Bohemia and Moravia had been under Austrian rule, while Slovakia and Sub-Carpathian Ruthenia had been part of Hungary. Demographic and economic factors made for yet more differences. Then there was, as outlined earlier, the impact of the migration of Jews from Poland (or rather Galicia) to the adjacent regions of northeastern Slovakia and Sub-Carpathian Ruthenia.

The most beneficial conditions, at least from the economic and political as well as demographic standpoints, existed in Bohemia and Moravia. By the beginning of the twentieth century large areas of the Bohemian Crownlands had been industrialized. Jewish participation in this process had been considerable and a widely based Jewish middle class, akin to that in Germany, came into being rapidly. Jews entered the realms of middle management and the bureaucracy, while remaining involved in such traditional Jewish pursuits as banking, retailing and the free professions. As in Germany too, there was a massive shift of Jewish population from the small towns and villages to the cities and larger industrial towns. Large numbers of Bohemian Jews joined their non-Jewish neighbours in flocking to Prague, Brno (Brünn) and Moravská Ostrava (Mährisch Ostrau) as well as the Imperial capital Vienna. Whole communities in the country areas, especially of Bohemia, practically ceased to exist. By the turn of the century over a third of the Jews in Bohemia (92,746) lived in Prague and its immediate environs, while nearly a quarter of those in Moravia lived in Brno. Even though many Jews who continued to live in the countryside led marginal existences as small shopkeepers or peddlers and most who resided in the cities had modest incomes, the majority of the Jewish population of the Bohemian Crownlands had incomes which were at levels to be classified as middle class and were certainly above those of the population as a whole. Not surprisingly the level of educational attainment was correspondingly high, with an increasing number of Jewish young people going on to institutions of learning beyond the secondary level.

In so far as legal emancipation made much of the above in the first place possible, and the first steps towards Jewish toleration would not have taken place without the important role played by Jews in the nascent capitalist economy of the Bohemian Crownlands, economic and political circumstances were for the Jews intimately intertwined. Despite its halting and sometimes ambivalent nature, the process of emancipation (finally completed in 1867) had helped bring the Jews of Bohemia and Moravia to the threshold of the modern era. Hand in hand with improving economic conditions and the Jewish enlightenment, which took an early hold in the Bohemian Crownlands, it facilitated the acculturation, urbanization and embourgeoisement of Bohemian and Moravian Jewry to the point that the famous Prague-Jewish novelist Franz Kafka could write in the much-quoted letter to his father:

> *You really had brought some traces of Judaism with you from the ghetto-like village community; it was not much and it dwindled a little more in the city and during your military service; but still, the impressions and memories of your youth did just about suffice for*

some sort of Jewish life . . . there was still Judaism enough, but it was too little to be handed on to the child; it was all dribbled away while you were passing it on . . . The whole thing is, of course, no isolated phenomenon. It was much the same with a large section of transitional Jewry, which had migrated from the still comparatively devout countryside to the cities.

Yet, for all their economic success and high degree of acculturation (some would argue that the Jews of Prague and Brno had come even further in dissociating themselves from Jewish religious practice than their counterparts in Germany), there was a certain incongruousness in the situation of the Jews of Bohemia and Moravia. They had for the most part acculturated towards the German element in the two Crownlands, who themselves were an increasingly embattled minority, instead of toward the Czech majority, amongst whom they mostly lived.

As a consequence, and also because of their economic power, they were regarded with growing resentment by the politically and economically emerging Czechs. In their eyes the Jews were allies of German political oppression as well as socio-economic exploiters and competitors. It did not matter much that from 1890 (the first census in which they were asked to do so) onwards the majority of the Jews registered their 'language of daily use' (*Umgangssprache*) as Czech and that at election time they voted for Czech candidates. For the Czechs it was much more important that the majority of Jews had opted for German culture and that the upper strata of the Jewish bourgeoisie were seemingly part of the power structure which ruled the Bohemian Crownlands as well as the German half of the Dual Monarchy.

German antisemitism, no matter how intense it became under the pressure of developments in Austria and Germany, on the other hand, tended only to affect Jews indirectly. For the most part, it did not prevent them from reading German newspapers and books or sending their children to German schools and universities. Put simply, the majority of Jews in the Bohemian Crownlands took their German cultural assimilation (acculturation) for granted and welcomed the positive advantages it brought them in terms of career opportunities and wider cultural horizons. They could, what is more, continue to exist as culturally assimilated Germans without identifying themselves with German nationalism, whereas to become Czech would have entailed not simply the adoption of the Czech language, but also a wholehearted commitment to the aims and ideals of the Czech national movement. This would have been a daunting task, even in the best of circumstances.

Even though by the turn of the century the situation in Slovakia bore some similarity to the one outlined above, it remained significantly different at least until the advent of war. For one thing, under Hungarian rule Slovakia remained both politically and economically underdeveloped. The vast majority of the population continued to be engaged in agriculture under semi-feudal conditions and, thanks to the limited system of suffrage, without the right to vote. A nationally aware Slovak middle class, as such, hardly existed. Consequently, the cultural nationalism of the Slovaks continued to have little scope to develop a political dimension as it did in Bohemia and Moravia.

While the Hungarian Government's liberal policy of magyarization ostensibly provided an impetus for Jewish assimilation, the general economic backwardness of the region and the size as well as compactness of the Jewish community, especially in the north-east where large number of Jews from neighbouring Galicia had settled, meant that its potential was never fully realized. The life-style of the handful of magyarized Jewish families who played such a dominant role in the little industrial development that took place in Slovakia remained in sharp contrast to that of their co-religionists who lived in the villages and small towns as inn-keepers, petty traders, middlemen and peddlers, steeped in religious orthodoxy and tradition. Even so, in the 1910 census over half, or 76,553, of the Jews in Slovakia entered their nationality as Magyar on the basis of mother tongue. Only 4,956 registered themselves as Slovak or Czech, while 58,300 indicated their nationality as German, of whom a high percentage were presumably Yiddish-speakers.

In this situation, it was hardly surprising that for economic, and to a lesser extent for national and religious, reasons popular resentment against the Jews was widespread in Slovakia. Yet, because of the generally underdeveloped state of Slovak political life, political antisemitism as such was slow to gain a foothold. The position of the Jews in Sub-Carpathian Ruthenia, who were to constitute the greatest concentration of Jewish population in the Czechoslovak Republic (15.4 per cent of the total inhabitants of the province), as already indicated above, was in some ways similar to that in northeastern Slovakia.

While there is no reason to suppose that anti-Jewish feeling did not exist there, until the period of Czechoslovak independence it was devoid of political dimension. The 'Jewish question' in Sub-Carpathian Ruthenia only started to develop in the 1920s and was as much concerned with the Jews' own adaptation to changing economic circumstances as with the problems of antisemitism and assimilation.

Romania

A more complex and diverse state of affairs than in Czechoslovakia existed in Romania, the only country in the region to have had its independence prior to the First World War. Pre-war and post-war Romania were, however, very different states. Before 1914 it comprised the territories of Moldavia, Wallachia and part of Dobrogea. Known as the Old Kingdom or the Regat, it was a nation-state with the overwhelming majority of its population being of Romanian nationality. All this changed as a consequence of Romania having joined the victorious Allied powers in 1918. The neighbouring lands with substantial Romanian population were annexed to the Regat. Included were the formerly Austrian Bukowina, formerly Russian Bessarabia, formerly Bulgarian Dobrogea and formerly Hungarian Transylvania (itself comprising the three regions of the Banat of Temeshvar, Siebenbürgen and Crisana-Maramures). In end effect, Romania was transformed from a small country with a largely ethnically homogeneous population to the second largest country of East Central Europe with all the problems of a multi-national state.

The diversity of ethnic origin and previous hegemony was naturally reflected in the composition of the country's Jewish community. It was not merely a matter of distinguishing between the Jews who had lived in the pre-war kingdom and each of the new territories, but within each of these units there were several, essentially different communities. The relatively small number of Jews in Wallachia concentrated in the capital, Bucharest, amongst whom there was a small but wealthy and influential group of families of Sephardic origin. As one might expect, this community was characterized by a high degree of acculturation, despite considerable Romanian antisemitism resulting from the important role Jews, as elsewhere, played in the commercial life of the country which they had traditionally dominated together with the Greeks, Germans and other non-Romanians.

Moldavian Jewry, on the other hand, presented a picture much more along the lines of the Polish model. Not only had many Jews come from formerly Polish territories (mostly those annexed by the Russian Empire to the north), but they were culturally and religiously within the orbit of Galician Jewry. Barely touched by the *Haskalah*, Chassidism and Orthodoxy held sway over the 160,000 odd Jews in the province, most of whom lived in the countryside and earned their livelihoods as intermediaries in the primitive agricultural economy. As in the eastern reaches of Poland some Jews even functioned as *arendars*, or leaseholders, of the Roman nobility. Culminating in the great peasant revolt of 1907, when pogrom-like conditions prevailed in the Moldavian countryside, the Jews in the province were faced with mounting and increasingly virulent antisemitism. Lacking for the most part citizenship or any of the other accoutrements of emancipation, the position of the Jews of pre-war Romania in political terms was comparable only to that of the Jews of the Russian Empire.

This contrasted sharply with the situation of the Jews in the territories which had prior to independence been under the rule of the Habsburgs. Except in historic Transylvania and the Banat of Temeshvar and the cities, most notably German-speaking Cernáuti (Czernowitz), conditions were similar to those in Galicia and Sub-Carpathian Ruthenia. Yiddish was not only the *lingua franca* but the native language of the greater part of the Jewish population of these territories, although in those which had formerly been under Hungarian rule there had been considerable acculturation, with many Jews speaking fluent Magyar. Even though in Czernowitz as well as in the cities of Transylvania the Reform movement made some inroads, Chassidism and Orthodoxy prevailed. So it was that two of the most influential Chassidic courts were located in Romania, at Satmar in Mamures and Satagura in the Bukowina.

Hungary

In a variety of ways the experience of Hungarian Jewry before the First World War contrasted significantly with that of the rest of the Jews in East Central Europe. By and large the Jews of Hungary had been, in a manner of speaking, co-opted to the ruling Magyar nationality. They had become politically as well as culturally assimilated to an extent that cannot be readily compared to any other country in Central Europe, perhaps not even Germany.

This situation was the consequence of the unique political and socio-economic conditions prevailing in Hungary since 1867, when a compromise (the so-called *Ausgleich*) was arrived at between the

Hungarian nobility and the Habsburgs whereby the Crownlands of St Stephen (pre-war Hungary) had the practical equivalent of 'Home Rule' from Vienna. Magyar political and cultural autonomy having been achieved, in turn left no doubt in which direction Jewish acculturation would proceed. But the ruling Hungarian gentry by actually welcoming and encouraging Jews into their midst engendered a form of acculturation which seemingly went beyond anywhere else in Central Europe. True, the ruling elite in Hungary may have had the ulterior motive of accepting Jews along with other non-Magyars into their ranks because of the need to bolster their hold over the millions of non-Magyar peoples (Slovaks, Croats, Ukrainians and Romanians).

The condominium, as it were, that developed between the Magyar ruling elite and the Jews of Hungary also encompassed the economic sphere in which the Jewish role was at least as significant as in the other societies of East Central Europe. Jews were not only agents and lessees of the Magyar landed nobility but also constituted, for all practical purposes, the industrial and commercial bourgeoisie of the country. With the rising rate of economic growth, the Jewish population of Hungary became increasingly urbanized and centred in the capital Budapest – 45 per cent by 1920. The remaining 55 per cent for the most part lived in country towns like Stephen Roth's birthplace Gyoengyoes in the northeastern part of the country, and such small cities as Miskolc, Debrecen or Szeged. In effect, this meant that a fairly high proportion of Hungarian Jewry was still concentrated in country areas where they very often led marginal existences as intermediaries in the rural economy. Steeped in Orthodoxy and Chassidism, their life-styles were virtually indistinguishable from those of their co-religionists across in the formerly Hungarian territories of Slovakia, Sub-Carpathian Ruthenia and Transylvania with whom they had been united before the dissolution of the Habsburg Monarchy. As was the case with these latter communities, the Polish roots of the Jews of northeastern Hungary were clearly in evidence, even though they were to a significant degree covered over by Magyar acculturation.

In the absence of a nationality question, the factor besides socio-economic standing which, nevertheless, divided Hungarian Jewry was religion. Ever since 1868 it was, namely, divided into two rival camps – the Reform or 'Neolog' and the Orthodox. An off-shoot of the Orthodox, called the 'status quo', which tried to find a middle way between the two extremes, eventually also came into existence. To call them extremes is perhaps somewhat inappropriate, since the

Austria–Hungary
© C A Macartney and A W Palmer 1962

actual differences in religious practice were not as marked as between the Orthodox and Reform elsewhere in Europe, especially Germany. Essentially, the split occurred as a consequence of the Orthodox leadership's refusal to accept any kind of reform in the first place. Elsewhere, notably in Bohemia and Moravia as well as in many parts of Germany, certain changes in the liturgy were adopted – such as for example the introduction of the organ for certain occasions, and sermons in German – which had broad consensus and allowed the Jewish communities in question to remain unified, but not in Hungary where the Orthodox Rabbinate held steadfastly to the position that all forms of modernization were inherently wrong.

Not surprisingly, and in spite of the fact that Neolog communities had already prior to 1914 been established in such centres of Orthodoxy as Miskolc, Bratislava (Pressburg; Possony) or Kosice (Kaschau; Kassa), the Orthodox remained most firmly entrenched in the small towns, especially in the northeast, along the borders with what became Czechoslovakia and Romania. Here the

'Polish' roots of a large segment of Hungarian Jewry were clearly in evidence.

Even though the majority of all Jews in Hungary, regardless of religious affiliation, took their acculturation for granted, the split between the Orthodox and Neolog communities had the consequence that Hungarian Jewry was essentially incapable of united action. It also resulted in a higher percentage of the Jewish population than anywhere else in Central Europe defining its identity in religious as opposed to ethnic terms, steadfastly regarding themselves as 'Magyars of the Jewish persuasion'. It was no wonder then that prior to World War One Zionism made hardly any headway in Hungary, even though two of the movement's leading figures – Theodor Herzl and Max Nordau – were Hungarian Jews.

However favourable the general pre-war environment may have been for Jews, there was no lack of antisemitism. But it was primarily of the social variety and hardly affected the lives of the majority of Hungarian Jews, mostly manifesting itself in the upper reaches of society. Even when a political antisemitic movement emerged in the 1880s, it failed to achieve a popular base. The peasantry was not interested in the 'Jewish question' and the Christian bourgeoisie had not yet developed to the point that it was inclined to resent the commanding position of the Jews in commerce and industry. Also, neither the Catholic nor Protestant churches ever got involved in the antisemitic movement and the Government did its best to exercise a protective role *vis-à-vis* the Jews.

For the Jews of Hungary these were obviously halcyon days. And yet, although very few people realized it, the end was not far away. The great watershed in the history of Hungarian Jewry, as elsewhere in East Central Europe, came in the wake of the First World War, when the old order fell apart. In answering the classic Jewish question, 'Was the war good for the Jews or bad for the Jews?' one would have to reply 'Bad'.

The Years between the Wars and of the Holocaust

Hungary

In Trianon Hungary, as the post-war Magyar state was known after the treaty which called it into being, the unspoken assumption which underpinned the relationship of the Jews to the Hungarian elite was no longer operative. With the loss of all the non-Magyar lands of the Crown of Stephen, the Jews lost their function as agents of magyarization. Moreover, whereas in the expansionist days of the pre-war period the Jews' role in the economy was seen in generally positive terms, in the less advantageous inter-war period their domination of economic life was viewed with resentment and seen as harmful. The aristocracy, many of whom had lost estates in Czechoslovakia, Romania or Yugoslavia and found their status threatened by the demise of the Habsburg monarchy, saw the Jews as interlopers who were potential competitors.

Far more than real or imagined economic woes, what shaped the attitude of the old Hungarian elite towards the Jews in the immediate post-war period was the one hundred day ill-fated Soviet regime of Béla Kun. Not only was Kun himself of Jewish origin, but so were 21 out of 26 of his ministers. Launched by a coalition of right-wing anti-Bolsheviks and old-style liberals under the naval hero Admiral Miklós Horthy, the ensuing white terror which followed the overthrow of the Kun regime in 1919 could, therefore, almost not help taking on a decidedly antisemitic character. For the first time anti-Jewish excesses were not suppressed and the country was inundated with antisemitic propaganda. Suddenly, Hungarian Jewry felt the full brunt of antisemitism, even if much of the invective was directed against the supposed wave of recent arrivals from Poland.

At least in the short run, however, the fact that the Horthy regime chose to direct its attacks solely against the hoards of 'Galicians' who had purportedly invaded Hungary facilitated the resurrection of the old condominium between the Jewish and Hungarian elites. Jews continued not only to serve as lessees of the magnates' estates and take aristocrats into their firms, but also to lend their financial support to the regime. As a consequence, their fate became linked to a maintenance of the *status quo*, a quasi-restored version of the old pre-war order. For, in the eyes of most Jews it was certainly preferable to a regime of the extreme right

The Peace Settlement 1919–23
© C A Macartney and A W Palmer 1962

which they felt would succeed Horthy, and about whose antisemitic programme there was no secret.

Not that the Horthy regime was above introducing anti-Jewish measures. In the wake of the signing of the humiliating Trianon Treaty of 1920 which acknowledged the annexation of formerly Hungarian territory by the successor states, legislation was enacted limiting the attendance at universities by the various 'races and nationalities' according to their proportion of the general population. Although the word 'Jew' was never mentioned in the law, it was abundantly clear against whom that statute was directed.

Also telling was the reaction of the Hungarian Jewish leadership to the law's enactment: they did nothing. It took the British Jewish Board of Deputies and French Alliance Israélite to launch a protest at the League of Nations which the representatives of Hungarian Jewry did not even join. Their feeling was, quite simply, that outside interference would only make matters worse: the antisemitic argument that Jews were a cosmopolitan people acting in concert with Hungary's enemies would be reinforced.

Of course, the position of the Hungarian Jewish leadership was morally untenable, and in the long term highly dangerous because it set a pattern of behaviour that was to continue into the 1930s and 1940s. On the other hand, they had no other choice but to cooperate with the moderate right-wing establishment as the only political grouping in the country which stood a chance of averting a takeover by the avowedly antisemitic far right. It was in the last analysis a sorrowful matter of choosing the lesser of two evils.

Sadly, however, the impossibility of the situation revealed itself soon enough, thanks largely to factors completely out of the control of the Hungarian Jewish leadership or, for that matter, the moderate right. At the root of this turn of events was the world economic crisis of the 1930s which hit the agriculturally- and export-based Hungarian economy badly. The peasantry was severely affected as were university graduates who even before the onset of bad times had difficulties in finding suitable employment.

Finally, in 1932 Admiral Horthy yielded to pressure from the extreme right and appointed Gyula Gömbös to lead a new Hungarian Government. The new prime minister was an open racist whose aim it had been since the 1920s to rid Hungary of Jewish influence. With the emergence of the openly fascist Arrow Cross Party, under the leadership of Ferenc Salaszi, Gömbös thus seemed to the Hungarian Jewish leadership, just as, earlier, his more moderate predecessor Bethlen had appeared, the lesser of two evils.

The ark in the old synagogue in
Sopron, Hungary, believed to
have been built in 1350.
Beth Hatefutsoth

One of the great rabbinical figures from Hungary's past – 'Hatam Sofer' – Rabbi Moshe Sofer (1762-1839). An oil painting based on a drawing by Ber Frank Halevi in the mid-19th century.
Jewish Museum, Budapest

The loyalty of Jews to the place of their domicile has always been as notable as their devotion to their religion. Here King Ferdinand I of Hungary visits the Jewish school in Poszóny (Germ: Pressburg) – now Bratislava in Czechoslovakia – in 1830. From a copper engraving by Julius Weissenberg.
Jewish Museum, Budapest

**Delegates to the Jewish
Congress in Budapest of 1868.**
Jewish Museum, Budapest

The community prospered in the 19th century. Some very greatly indeed. This is the Singer family of Budapest in 1900.
Beth Hatefutsoth

Above:
Unlike in the Second World
War, the conflict of 1914-18
frequently set Jew against Jew. It
was quite conceivable that a
Jewish 'Tommy' fought a Jewish
'Fritz' to the death in the
trenches. Here, Jewish
Hungarian soldiers are seen
celebrating the Jewish New Year
of Rosh Hashanah on the front
in the autumn of 1916.
Ms L Herdan, England

Left:
To some, prosperity was owning
a shop. These are Jewish-owned
shops in Budapest in 1890.
Jewish Museum, Budapest

Jews were astonishingly active in the revolutionary movement that followed the downfall of the Austro-Hungarian Empire in 1918. Among these members of the Revolutionary Ruling Council were (second from right, front row) Jeno Hamburger and (next to him) Béla Kun, Jeno Varga, Tibor Szamuely, Béla Szanto. Second from left is Otto Korvin.

Museum of the Hungarian Labour Movement, Budapest

Chassidic Jews after morning
prayers in a village in Eastern
Hungary c.1920.
Kibbutz Lohamei Haghetaot

The ambition to live one day in
Palestine meant preparing for
that day. The Hashomer Hatzair
Zionist movement provided
agricultural training in Bicske,
Hungary (1929).
Zsoldos family, Israel

There were frequently quota
regulations imposed on the
number of Jews allowed to go to
Hungary's universities. Those
who did 'make' it, however, had
their own Jewish Students
Union. This was a students'
union ball in Budapest in 1930.
Agi Heller, Israel

Children attending the first Jewish children's centre in Budapest, opened in the community building in the Hungarian capital in 1935.
Nobel family, Israel

Many Hungarian Jews attended yeshivot, or talmudical colleges, like this one at Vac in 1937.
Dr Abraham Fuchs, Israel

The war had begun, but the
Holocaust had not yet started to
bite in Hungary. This was a
performance of a play at the
Goldmark Hall for culture in
Budapest in 1940.
Vera Rosza, London

Indeed, much to the surprise of everyone, soon after assuming power he came to an agreement with the Neolog community of Budapest, which presumably included financial support, and made what amounted to a complete ideological about-face on the Jewish question. As long as he remained in power, Hungary acceded to pressure from neither Germany nor the Arrow Cross and other elements on the extreme right at home to introduce its own equivalent of the anti-Jewish Nuremberg Laws or revive the legislation of the 1920s which implemented the *numerus clausus*.

By 1938, however, the Gömbös government fell from power and the new Premier, Daranyi, gave in to the demands of the Germans as well as the Arrow Cross. Legislation was drafted and quickly passed severely limiting Jewish participation in virtually all aspects of economic and public life. In effect, the 'first Jewish law of May 1938', as it was called, imposed a *numerus clausus* on almost the whole of Hungarian society, thereby bringing to an end Jewish emancipation. But, there was still worse to come.

Within a year, despite some opposition from the left and liberals as well as some prominent old conservatives who felt that the legislation was going too far, the Hungarian Parliament passed the notorious 'second Jewish law' which came into effect in May 1939. While outwardly resembling the anti-Jewish legislation introduced by the Nazis in Germany in the years since 1933, it was still not entirely racialist in its definition of who was a Jew, and it allowed for at least a measure of Jewish activity in the economy instead of choking it completely as had happened in Germany. Because of inefficiency, corruption or a combination of both on the part of the local officials charged with enforcing the law, there was a general weakening of its impact. At the end of the day, however, the Jews of Hungary had been deprived of their emancipation, and with the outbreak of war there seemed little hope of its being recovered.

The policy of the assimilationist leadership in Budapest was finally bankrupt. All displays of Magyar patriotism were useless and demeaning. Their hope of supporting the old conservatives to stave off the far right had proved futile. Under pressure from the increasingly popular Arrow Cross and their German allies, even most of their erstwhile allies amongst the old right found the implementation of antisemitic measures unavoidable. An amalgam of antisemitism and opportunism, moreover, assured a popular base in favour of the legislation once it was implemented.

Still, even after her entry into the war the internal conflict over the resolution of the Jewish question in Hungary continued.

Predictably, it remained a matter of the Germans and their domestic right-wing allies trying to push the Government to take ever more radical action against the Jews. Thus, as late as the fateful year of 1944, the Regent, Admiral Horthy, who still retained considerable leeway in domestic affairs, was able to write Hitler that he was determined to solve the Jewish question in Hungary without having to use 'brutal and inhumane' methods.

In the end, as we well know, it was the Nazis and their Hungarian allies who had their day and not Horthy. The deportations got under way within months of the German occupation of March 1944 and reached their height in the period between May 5th and June 7th when 300,000 Hungarian Jews were deported to the death camps of the East, although Horthy, who retained some powers under the German occupation, was able to prevent the deportation of the Jews of Budapest. Even earlier, between 1941 and 1942, the Hungarian authorities had forcibly expelled thousands of supposed 'Galicians' to Poland where almost all were killed by the Germans, and thousands of Jews along with Serbs were brutally murdered by Hungarian forces in the Novy Sad region of what had formerly been Yugoslavia. Additionally, thousands of Jewish men were forced to serve in the infamous labour battalions of the Hungarian Army on the Eastern Front, where many helplessly perished.

The assimilationist ideology of the Hungarian Jewish leadership was discredited. Its policy of cooperating to the fullest extent possible with successive Hungarian Governments, despite their implementing increasingly more severe antisemitic legislation and measures, lay in ruins. On the other hand, posterity will have to judge whether in so doing they did not indeed save lives.

Czechoslovakia

Although in Czechoslovakia too a *modus vivendi* had been found in the relations between the Jewish minority and country's ruling elite, it had a decidedly different character than in Hungary. A typical liberal admixture of principles and pragmatism, it was born of the realization that failing to combat antisemitism would have negative consequences for the young state's image with the Western allies. At least for as long as President Masaryk (who had already taken a courageous stance against the ritual murder myth in the famous Hilsner affair at the turn of the century) was at the helm of state, moreover, there was a sense amongst politicians as well as the population at large that Czechoslovakia's treatment of Jews was a touchstone of her commitment to democratic values and the rule of law.

This commitment was put to the test in the initial period after the founding of the state when antisemitic violence, both in the former Bohemian Crownlands and Slovakia, threatened to become a widespread instead of a limited occurrence. Even Czech political leaders who had previously made their anti-Jewish views perfectly clear were now counselling restraint to their fellow countrymen, lest the image of Czechoslovakia be tarnished in eyes of the Allies in whose hands the fate of the new state seemed to hang. Specifically, the Czechoslovak delegation at the Paris Peace Conference was anxious to avoid the imposition of a clause similar to ones forced upon the Poles and Romanians recognizing the Jews as a separate national minority, a step which would have opened the Pandora's box of national minority status for all the state's ethnic groups, most notably the Germans and Hungarians.

Intertwined with these events was the establishment on 22 October 1918, six days before Czechoslovak independence was declared, of the Jewish National Council in Prague with the declared aim of representing the interests of the Jews with the authorities of the new state. The Council, in effect, also became the organ through which President Masaryk's notions of Jewish national rights came to be expressed. The interests of the Council and the Czechoslovak Government seem to have become so intertwined that it probably even led the former to go along with the suspension of the publication at the beginning of December 1918 of the two Prague-German dailies, *Bohemia* and *Prager Tagblatt*, for reporting a recent outburst of anti-German and anti-Jewish unrest. For its part, the Government was obviously anxious to keep a tight lid on the story, lest it give encouragement to similar excesses elsewhere in the Republic or damage its case with the Allies on the minorities issue.

It still came as a great disappointment to the representatives of the Council at the Paris Peace Conference when the Allies accepted the proposal of the head of the Czechoslovak delegation, Foreign Minister Eduard Benes, that the specifically 'Jewish clauses' of the Polish 'Model Treaty' should be removed from the version to be signed by his country. Neither the Jewish delegates themselves nor the intervention of Nahum Sokolov or the Anglo-Jewish leader Lucien Wolf managed to bring about a reversal of this decision. Not even the threat to mobilize Jewish opinion in the United States in favour of the clauses had any effect and a last-minute attempt to secure an intervention by Masaryk failed to materialize.

Benes remained steadfast in his position that for Czechoslovakia to accept specific provisions for the protection of Jewish rights would put her on a par with Poland and Romania, and this her treatment of the Jews did not warrant. It would, moreover, imply both a general lack of faith in the ability of the Czechoslovak authorities 'to respect certain human rights which are regarded as a matter of course' and a support for the Zionists against the assimilationists, which the Czechoslovak delegation did not feel it was in a position to do. Equally, Benes was concerned, as has been indicated earlier, lest a concession to the Jews would lead to similar demands from the national minorities in the Czechoslovak state generally.

The Allies accepted Benes' proposals, first of all because they agreed with him that it would not be feasible to turn Czechoslovakia into a Central European Switzerland, with each national group guaranteed some form of political, territorial and cultural autonomy. They moreover sincerely believed that Czechoslovakia, as far as the Jewish problem was concerned, represented a different case from Romania or especially Poland. If the British reports on the subject are an indication, they were convinced that antisemitic unrest had not taken place in Czechoslovakia on anywhere near the scale on which it had occurred in Poland and that the Czechoslovak Government's policy towards the Jews was above reproach.

While this assessment of the situation was essentially correct, it did not reveal the whole story. Czechoslovakia continued to be plagued by anti-Jewish agitation and excesses until after the peace treaties had been signed, even if the attacks that did take place were much less frequent and on a much smaller scale than in either Poland or Romania. The fact still remained, however, that the situation was potentially volatile, especially in Slovakia where the Jews were wrongly blamed for acting as a 'fifth column' during the invasion of the troops of Béla Kun's Hungarian Soviet Republic (1 May-23 June 1919) in Czechoslovakia. Fearful of what might happen, Dr Chaim Weizmann, acting on behalf of the Zionist Organization in London, wrote to the Czechoslovak authorities on 9 July 1919 to express his concern and remind them of the probably negative effect on Western opinion if the Government failed to keep the situation under control. Replying, some three months later and three weeks after the peace treaties had been signed, the Minister for Slovakia, Vavro Srobar, rejected out of hand any allegation that the Czechoslovak authorities had been remiss in maintaining public order in Slovakia. On the contrary, he wrote to

Weizmann, it was the Jews themselves who bore the ultimate responsibility for the attacks. Their behaviour both during and after the war had, in his eyes, been nothing short of provocative. One is inevitably led to wonder whether Srobar would not have couched his allegations in more careful language or omitted them altogether, had he replied to Weizmann before rather than after the treaties had been signed.

Although the situation in Slovakia remained calm, in Bohemia and to a lesser extent in Moravia there was more violence. In November 1920 a wave of anti-German unrest spread from western Bohemia to Prague as well as Brno and Prostejov in Moravia. The situation in Prague was so bad that after the Jewish Town Hall had been ransacked by a Czech mob the US Embassy allowed the American flag to be hoisted over the building in an attempt to protect the Jewish refugees from Galicia being housed there temporarily.

While these later disturbances were the last instances of anti-Jewish violence in the First Czechoslovak Republic, antisemitism remained a strong political and social undercurrent until the country's demise in 1938/39. Up to the 1930s it erupted, as it were, in the right-wing nationalist press and in Czech and Slovak literature as well as in the form of the occasional anti-Jewish remark at the local pub or the National Assembly. It was an antisemitism which the Czechoslovak leader quite rightly termed 'tolerable' ('erträglich'). It appeared so especially when compared to the conditions Jews had to endure in the rest of Central and Eastern Europe. The Jews of inter-war Czechoslovakia, for the most part, had to suffer neither a barrage of antisemitic propaganda and abuse, as in Germany or Austria, the danger of physical attack, as in Poland or Romania, nor the humiliation of the *numerus clausus*, as in Hungary.

This did not mean, however, that the Jews of inter-war Czechoslovakia did not face many of the same trials and tribulations as their co-religionists in the other states of East Central Europe. Throughout most of the country they were under constant pressure from the majority population to relinquish German or Hungarian in favour of Czech or Slovak language and culture. In those areas and towns where there were clear Czech or Slovak majorities this began to happen quite naturally as the knowledge of these languages actually became or was perceived as a vital pre-requisite for employment in the public as well as the private sectors. We see for example that by the late 1920s and 1930s increasing numbers of

Jews are enrolled at Czech as well as Slovak secondary schools, which was certainly previously not the case. The same was true a bit later on at the Czech and Slovak institutions of higher education.

The Jews of Czechoslovakia also faced increasing pressure in the economic sphere, notably in their role as intermediaries in the rural economy. As elsewhere in Europe by the late nineteenth century cooperatives had begun performing many of the functions in the countryside which had previously been the exclusive purview of the Jews, whether it was providing seed, selling cattle, purchasing produce or running village pubs. In the first Czechoslovak Republic these activities were given further impetus thanks largely to the efforts of the Agrarian Party which became one of the leading political forces in the new state. Trusts were set up which effectively took the trade in various commodities, such as sugar beet, hides and hops, increasingly out of the hands of private merchants, most of whom were Jews. Putting any antisemitic aspect aside, the end effect was the same: Jews in the rural areas of the Republic found their livelihoods severely endangered or eliminated altogether. As a consequence of land reform, both in Slovakia and Sub-Carpathian Ruthenia, some Jews also lost their positions as estate managers. Although such measures were clearly part of a broader process of economic change, behind their implementation was the notion that the intermediary role of the Jews in the rural economy was in itself harmful. This allowed the Agrarians and their allies on the right to adopt a stance that was implicitly rather than explicitly antisemitic.

In Slovakia, where political, economic, and demographic conditions were much closer to those in Poland and Romania, antisemitism took on a much more overt role in political life than it did in Bohemia and Moravia. By the mid-1930s the political landscape became dominated by right-wing nationalist movements associated with the Catholic Church which made no secret of their desire to solve the 'Jewish question' along similar lines to Germany, from whom the more extreme elements received help and encouragement. Thus, it was to be expected that the Nazi invasion of March 1939 which brought an end to Czechoslovak independence would lead to the creation of a puppet Slovak state and that one of its first legislative acts would be a 'Jewish law', similar to the one implemented at about the same time in Hungary, which was specifically intended to bring about the elimination of the Jews from the political and economic life of the country. After the outbreak of war matters only got worse, with further restrictive legislation, again similar to that enacted by the Hungarians. Unlike

Inside the Altneuschul. Etching
by E M Lilien, early 20th
century.
Beth Hatefutsoth

**Shops in the former ghetto of
Prague, late 19th century.**
Yivo Institute, New York

**The Jewish cemetery in Prague at
the turn of the century. It has
changed little since then.**
The Hulton Picture Company

The Josefstädterstrasse in the Prague ghetto, early 20th century.
The Hulton Picture Company

The synagogue in the small town of Huncovec (Germ: Hunsdorf; Hung: Hunfalva). The North Slovakian town had a leading yeshiva (talmudical college). This synagogue was built in classical style in 1821.

Beth Hatefutsoth – L B Gassner, Haifa

The Orthodox synagogue in Lucenec (Hung: Losonc) Slovakia, 1935. It was built in 1862.

Lea Kartohvil, Holon, Israel

Jews were amongst the leading
cultural figures of pre-war
Czechoslovakia, the most notable
of whom was the writer Franz
Kafka. This is the path leading to
the primary school which Kafka
attended.
Jan Parik, USA

The Lucenec Synagogue in Slovakia. It was built in 1925 by Lipot Baumhorn, one of the foremost synagogue architects of the period.
Beth Hatefutsoth – L B Gassner, Haifa

There was no stronger association with Zionism than that of the youth. Here are members of the 'Young Maccabi' together with Maccabi athletes in the town of Zilina in 1935. They pose proudly with the Young Maccabi flag.
Beth Hatefutsoth

Zionism was one of the bedrocks
of pre-war European Jewry.
These are employees of the
Bratislava Eretz Israel Office in
about 1938.
Jan Weill, Israel

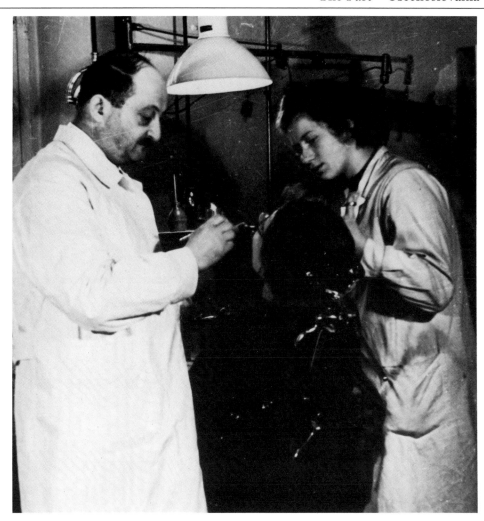

Part of the great deception wrought by the Nazis — the idea that life was going on as normal for the Jews of Czechoslovakia. This is a propaganda picture, of a Jewish dentist in Prague.
Wiener Library

Another propaganda picture which shows a Prague Jewish kindergarten at play.
Wiener Library

The spirit of the Jews who
survived the Holocaust in
Czechoslovakia was still strong.
This picture was taken at a
seminar organized by Jewish
Czech troops during Chanukah,
1945 at Teplice (Teplitz-
Schönau).
Beth Hatefutsoth

their Hungarian enemies and neighbours, however, the Slovak Government was unequivocal in its execution of Nazi Jewish policy. Led by the notorious fascist-like Hlinka Guard, charged with the implementation of government policy by the clerical regime of Father Tiso, about three-quarters of the Jews of Slovakia were finally rounded up and deported to extermination camps in the spring and summer of 1942. Deportations were halted, partly through the intervention of the Catholic Church and partly as a consequence of bribes and promises of financial payments made to Slovak officials, until the German occupation following the uprising of 1944. In the end, some 5,000 Slovak Jews came out of hiding and about 10,000 returned (most of whom had been deported in 1944 from territory previously ceded to Hungary) as survivors of the death and labour camps.

The future of Czechoslovak Jewry did not always look as bleak as it did in the late 1930s. Despite the initial period of unrest and certain underlying problems in their dealings with the various ethnic groups which comprised independent Czechoslovakia, the Jews had seemed to find a *modus vivendi* not only in their relationship to the new state but in their attempt to forge a new identity within society. The two were necessarily intertwined and had much to do with the relatively pluralist policies pursued by the Czechoslovak Government under President Masaryk and Prime Minister Benes.

As we have already seen, the first representative of the 'Jewish minority', the Jewish National Council in Prague, claimed to speak for the whole of Czechoslovak Jewry in pursuing its moderate national programme of recognition of the Jews as a nation, subsidies for Jewish schools and other cultural institutions as well as the democratization of Jewish communal bodies, while on an international level working towards the establishment of a Jewish National Home in Palestine. In order to achieve this programme, at a conference convened in 1919 it encouraged the formation of a Jewish Party. Intended to propagate the ideals of nationalism as well as defend the entire spectrum of Jewish interest, it hoped to attract wide support amongst the Jewish electorate of Czechoslovakia. For this reason, also, it tried to stay above the political fray, inviting into its midst Zionists and non-Zionists, socialists and non-socialists, as well as religious and secular Jews. Unlike in Poland where a similar attempt to weld a unified Jewish party failed because of the deep and bitter divisions that existed within the realm of Jewish politics, it achieved a moderate success in Czechoslovakia, at least in part because Jewish politics as such was still very much in its infancy, and in effect largely free of the deep ideological divisions that characterized Polish Jewish politics.

Its relative success at attracting voters (around 100,000 by the late 1920s), however, was more a consequence of the quandary or dilemma in which many Jews in Czechoslovakia still found themselves. In Bohemia and Moravia a large number of Jews could simply not bring themselves to vote for either Czech or German candidates. This was no doubt especially the case amongst Jews who were acculturated towards the German element, but felt that for one reason or another they could not vote for a German political candidate at election time. In Slovakia and Sub-Carpathian Ruthenia, where the situation was complicated by the opposition of the extreme Orthodox and Chassidism, the Jewish Party drew support not only from acculturated Magyar and Slovak elements but also from more moderate traditional Jews who, while not in any way inclined toward Zionism, felt that the best way of advancing their interests as Jews in the Czechoslovak Republic was by voting for the Jewish Party.

Although the Zionist cause, as such, did not win a mass following, there were signs of potential strength. Increasing numbers of Jewish young people joined the Zionist sports organizations and youth movements. This was even the case in the traditional regions of Slovakia and Sub-Carpathian Ruthenia, where compulsory secular education and the tensions caused by economic change combined in an atmosphere rife with nationalism and antisemitism as well as generational conflict to bring increasing numbers of young people into the Zionist camp. At the universities and other institutions of higher learning the Zionist student organizations gained in strength, but it was still by and large a matter of its adherents engaging in a personal search for identity and roots rather than planning seriously for *aliyah*. The situation only began to change in the late 1930s when Czechoslovak Jewry increasingly saw itself under the threat of mounting antisemitism at home and Nazism across the border in Germany.

It was, nevertheless, only with the demise of the First Czechoslovak Republic in the wake of Munich in 1938/39, and really only in Slovakia, that the antisemites could realize their aims. In what was left of Bohemia and Moravia (after March 1939 the so-called 'Protectorate of Bohemia and Moravia') as well as Sub-Carpathian Ruthenia, which was annexed by Hungary, anti-Jewish measures were imposed from without.

Had not the First Republic been torn apart by Hitler, the *modus vivendi* that had been established between, on the one hand, the Jews and, on the other, the Government and society of Czechoslovakia would in all likelihood have continued. With all its faults and high level of national tension, Czechoslovakia was still the only state of East Central Europe in which Jews could live as Jews and realize their full potential as citizens and members of society as a whole.

Romania

The same could not be said of Romania, where the antisemitism of the Regat (the pre-war kingdom) continued to be the bane of Jewish life in the country throughout its existence, even if the history of the inter-war period opened on a hopeful note. Although Romania under Allied pressure in a treaty of December 1919 agreed to confer citizenship on all 'Jews inhabiting any Romanian territory who do not possess another nationality', they were, as might have been the case with the Poles, required to sign an agreement promising absolute equality to all citizens 'without distinction as to race, language, or religion' which, furthermore, stated that there would be no discrimination in employment. The treaty also guaranteed the right of Romanian nationals of non-Romanian speech to use their language before the courts and to have schools of their own in districts where they represented a significant proportion of the population. Minorities were additionally allowed to maintain schools and other cultural institutions at their own expense. As far as the Jews of Romania were concerned, the treaty in effect granted them their emancipation.

As a consequence of territorial gains, there were now, however, many more Jews living in Romania than before the war; and this in itself became a problem. As early as in the deliberations which led to the treaty of December 1919, the leader of the Romanian Liberal Party, Ion Bratlianu, explained to President Woodrow Wilson that by clinging to certain professions and by their sheer numbers Jewish immigrants to Romania had given rise to a Jewish question in his country which, in his view, could only be compared to the 'Yellow Peril' in the United States. Even though he tempered his remarks (which became known to the Jewish Committee of Delegations to the Paris Peace Conference) somewhat by pointing to increasing Jewish assimilation and modernization of the economy, they left the Jewish leadership of Romania very concerned about the future.

Territorial changes 1938–41
© C A Macartney and A W Palmer 1962

They were correct, even if the Jews of Romania were spared the wave of anti-Jewish violence which engulfed Eastern Europe from the Ukraine to Czechoslovakia in the immediate post-war period, and the dominant Liberal Party initially pursued a policy of relative benevolence towards the Jews. Jewish refugees from the Soviet Union were allowed to settle in the neighbouring province of Bessarabia and some support was given to Jewish education. Citizenship, however, still remained a problem for many Jews, especially for those from the new regions of the Bukowina and Transylvania which had previously, it will be remembered, belonged to Austria-Hungary. Even though some were able to meet the residence requirements stipulated under the law and others bribed local officials to have them ignored, a good many were still left stateless. As elsewhere in East Central Europe, Jews encountered discrimination in the civil service and army.

Most disquieting, however, was the rising tenor of antisemitic agitation amongst the country's student population. In 1922, following a spate of anti-Jewish incidents, the authorities were even forced to close down the universities for a while and in 1926 a young Jew seeking admission to the University of Cernăuti (Czernowitz) was murdered by a Romanian student. The most serious disturbance did not occur at or near a university, but in 1927 at the largely non-Romanian Transylvanian town of Oradea Mare where a group of militant Romanian students gathered to assert the Romanian character of the region. Shortly after their arrival, rioting directed against Hungarians as well as Jews broke out. Two persons were killed and many wounded and a considerable amount of property, including two synagogues, was vandalized in the disorder.

On their way back to Bucharest and Iasi (Jassy) the students stopped off at Cluj (Klausenburg; Kolosvar) and several other towns where they behaved similarly. Significantly, in these excesses the Jews were identified with Hungarian and German minorities, whom the Romanian student militants viewed as ethnic oppressors. Similarly, in Bessarabia, after the abortive pro-Soviet coup, Jews came under attack for allegedly being Bolsheviks and pro-Russian.

The antisemitic character of student militancy made for serious disquiet amongst Romania's Jews, even though the Romanian Government took some action against the student militants, partly no doubt in response to international pressure (including from the Joint Foreign Committee of the Board of Deputies of British Jews) and did not initiate any anti-Jewish legislation as in Poland.

The real shift in Romanian politics came in the 1930s with the

increasing power of the old right led by newly-returned King Carol
and the growth of the radical right, notably the Iron Guard
movement under Corneliu Codreanu. Under the impact of the
Great Depression and the growing influence of Nazi Germany a
situation akin to that of Hungary developed whereby the traditional
conservatives were outflanked by fascist, pro-Nazi Iron Guard and
other elements of the radical right. After 1933 no small role was
played in these developments by the country's German minority
who quickly came under the influence of Nazism.

However ominous these developments in the political arena may
have been, they no doubt affected the lives of ordinary Jews less
than the worsening economic conditions brought on by the Great
Depression. The most hard hit area, at least as far as the Jews were
concerned, was Bessarabia which had suffered throughout the inter-
war period from being cut off from its traditional markets in Russia.

As far as the Jews were concerned, the new tenor of Romanian
politics was heralded by the passage in 1934, when the government
was still controlled by moderates, of a 'national work' law mandating
that 80 per cent of the employees in any firm must be 'Romanians'.
The so-called 'foreigners' whom the legislation aimed at excluding
from the work force were almost exclusively Jews who had failed to
be granted citizenship under Romania's biased nationality laws. It
was not of much solace to the Jews dismissed from their jobs in this
period that the liberal leadership continued to denounce the
antisemitism of the extreme right.

Worse, however, was still to come. King Carol, who was thought
by both many Jews and the antisemites to have a somewhat
benevolent attitude towards the Jews, because he had a Jewish
mistress and a rich Jewish friend, at the end of 1937 appointed an
avowedly antisemitic Government headed by two of the most
fervent patrons of the Iron Guard, Octavian Goga and Alexandru
Coza. The King's claims to foreigners that he had done so with the
ultimate aim of discrediting the far right gave little comfort to the
Jews of Romania, for no sooner did the Coza-Goga regime come to
power than it announced an anti-Jewish programme which made
that of the Gömbös Government pale by comparison. Jews were to
be excluded from the economy and higher education. All Jews who
had entered the country after the signing of the peace treaty were to
be expelled and all rights 'improperly granted' to Jews were to be
rescinded. Jewish newspapers and libraries were closed and various
professional organizations were forced or encouraged to expel their
Jewish members. While a hasty attempt was made to extend the

numerus clausus principle in the economy, actual legislation was passed requiring all Romanian Jews to prove the validity of their citizenship.

To the great relief of Romania's Jews, the Coza-Goga Government only lasted some two months. King Carol, supported by a group of conservative politicians intent on forestalling an outright takeover by the Iron Guard, arranged its demise. Within a matter of months the King installed himself in power, abolishing the constitution of 1923 and arranging for the assassination of Codreanu and several other key figures in the Iron Guard. For the next two years King Carol ruled supreme over a one-party corporatist state in an atmosphere in which he constantly had to prove himself to the increasingly popular and powerful extreme right, who believed first and foremost that he was a prisoner of the Jews.

As a consequence, the dictatorship of King Carol implemented a number of the anti-Jewish measures originally introduced by the Coza-Goga regime. Some 270,000 Jews were deprived of their citizenship, and Jews removed from their jobs during the *numerus clausus* were not re-hired by their employers. Plans were also made, but not implemented, to expel large numbers of so-called 'foreign Jews'.

The real change in King Carol's Jewish policy came in the wake of the loss of Bessarabia and the northern Bukowina to the Soviet Union under the Hitler-Stalin Pact of July 1940. A series of laws harsher than those instituted by the Hungarians, which they resembled, were quickly passed not only depriving all but a small group of privileged Jews of their basic rights, but for the first time defining the Jews as a race. Excluding Jews from virtually all aspects of public life, it also limited their ownership of property and prohibited intermarriage as well as conversion to Christianity. In one fell swoop the emancipation of Romanian Jewry came to a complete end.

Despite their harshness, the anti-Jewish measures instituted by Carol did not help placate his enemies on the right. Discredited as a consequence of Nazi *Realpolitik* which resulted not only in Romania's loss of Bessarabia and the northern Bukowina to the Soviets, but northern Transylvania to Hungary, in September 1940 the King was forced to abdicate and hand over the reins of government to a coalition of the Iron Guard and the military, which promptly formed the so-called National Legionary State with Marshal Antonescu at its head and the Iron Guard as its only legal party.

The Jewish quarter in Bucharest
at the turn of the century.
Dr Th. Lavi, Jerusalem

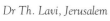

The Yiddish theatre was born in
Romania. Itzik Goldenberg in a
performance of 'Bar Kochba' at
the Jignitza Theatre, Bucharest,
1914.
Jewish Museum, Bucharest

**A bourgeois Jewish family in
Bucharest in the early years of
the century.**
Walter Zwiebel collection, Petah Tikvah

Jewish orphans in Bucharest after the First World War.
Yivo Institute, New York

Poverty was rife in the 1920s. Here are two war orphans having a hot meal at a soup kitchen run by the Joint Distribution Committee.
JDC Archive

A Jewish farmer and his son in
Petrovka, Bessarabia in the
1920s.
ICA Archives, Tel Aviv

Above:
The Zionist Centre in Kishinev,
Bessarabia, 1922.
Jabotinsky Institute, Tel Aviv

Left:
Building a new home. In 1920,
the Joint provides a loan for a
Jewish family to replace the
house which had been destroyed
in the First World War at
Campulung.
JDC Archive

A parade of Jewish Boy Scouts –
belonging to the Hashomer
Hatza'ir Zionist youth group – at
the Hebrew High School in Cluj
(Koloszwar), Transylvania, 1922.
Tel Itzhak, Masoah Archive

Wine-making was always an
honourable profession – and
when it was kosher wine, a holy
one, too. This was in the Jewish
colony of Petrovka in 1925.
ICA Archives, Tel Aviv

**A carpentry workshop of the He-
Halutz Zionist youth group in
Galatzi in 1922.**
Jewish Labour Movement Museum, Tel Aviv

They join hands to form a Shield
of David – highly symbolic for a
He-Halutz group in Kishinev,
Bessarabia, planning to emigrate
to Palestine in the 1920s.
Labour movement archives, Tel Aviv

**Girls at a vocational school in
Galatzi in the 1920s, run by
B'nai B'rith.**
Moshe Ussoskin, Jerusalem

Outskirts of a shtetl in the
Maramures region in the 1930s.
Yivo Institute, New York

Above:
A wedding in Botosani in the 1930s.
Centre for Research of Romanian Jewry, Jerusalem

Left:
Planning to go to Palestine – and preparing for it by learning farm work in Bazuci Bukowina, 1933.
Jabotinsky Institute, Tel Aviv

Children working in agriculture in the School of the Jewish Centre for Mother and Child, Bucharest in 1943. Somehow or other, life went on.
Yad Vashem, Jerusalem

The Chassidic rebbe of Vizhnitz, Rabbi Hayyim Meir Hager, with his followers in the 1930s.
Yad Vashem, Jerusalem

Now the onslaught against the Jews could begin in earnest. In late 1940, Jewish property was confiscated and a boycott of Jewish shops was organized. In January 1941, shortly before Antonescu with the support of the army ousted them from the Government, the Iron Guard organized a bloody pogrom in Bucharest.

Despite the elimination of the Iron Guard and the independence displayed by Antonescu (akin to that of Admiral Horthy in Hungary) in 'protecting' the Jews of the Regat and southern Transylvania from deportation to Nazi death camps, the condition of the Jews continued to deteriorate rapidly. In the Bukowina and Bessarabia, which were reconquered by Romanian and German troops in 1941, many were killed or expelled to conquered areas of the Ukraine where most met a similar fate. Nevertheless, by the time Romania changed sides after a coup led by the new King ousted Antonescu, 57 per cent of the pre-war Jewish population had survived the Holocaust. The course of the war, notably Hitler's defeats at Stalingrad and elsewhere in the Soviet Union, and the dogged determination of the Romanian authorities to maintain their independence from the Germans, go a long way to account for this circumstance, which sometimes appears incongruous given the triumph of extreme antisemitism.

Not surprisingly, for as long as Jewish political life was possible in Romania it reflected the increasing tenor of anti-Jewish feeling in the country. It could not help being shaped, as well, by the very diversity of the state's Jewish population, which much more than any of the others in East Central Europe was an agglomeration of several types of Jewries. At one end of the spectrum was the Union of Romanian Jews, or the UER, as it was known by its abbreviation. It represented the majority of Jews of the Regat and stood for a quasi-national identity which recognized the transformation of Romanian Jewry from a religious to an ethnic minority. Although it eschewed political as opposed to cultural assimilation, the UER was against the formation, as in Czechoslovakia, of a Jewish party, and consistently recommended to its followers that they vote for the political grouping which was most unfailing in support of Jewish rights, first the Liberals and then the Socialists.

Although Zionism was the single most powerful political movement in the new territories, much as in Poland it was split into several hostile factions. Opposing them were numerous other national and anti-national groupings, ranging from *Bundists* in Bessarabia and folkist nationalists in the Bukowina to Agudists and Chassidim in Transylvania. Clearly, these divisions were influenced by circumstances prevailing both before and after the war.

In some areas the incorporation into the Romanian state benefitted the rise of Zionism. This was especially true in Bessarabia, which had already had a strong Jewish nationalist tradition, but also in the former Austro-Hungarian territories of the Bukowina, where the end of Austrian tolerance and the diminishing role of German culture was especially traumatic, and Transylvania, where Magyar and to a lesser extent German acculturation lost their former attraction.

Given this high degree of diversity, it is hardly surprising that in Romania a Jewish political grouping was relatively slow in developing. The emergence in 1928 of a Jewish national club in parliament only came in the wake of increasing frustration on the part of Jewish nationalists from the new territories, who were fed up with being forced to support the Liberals who only vowed to uphold rights at election time. Although initially not supported by all Zionists, some of whom opposed anything but Palestine-oriented activism, by 1931 the club felt itself confident enough to form the Jewish Party of Romania and run a list of candidates of its own. After doing quite well at first, polling some 67,000 votes and winning five seats by 1932, less than a year later its electoral strength was cut by almost a half. At the end of the day, it was clear that the only reliable base of support for a Jewish national party in Romania was in the new territories. With the increase in antisemitism, moreover, most Jewish voters probably felt that their interests were ultimately best served by throwing in their lot with the traditional foes of antisemitism on the left, mainly the Socialists. On the other hand, outside parliament the UER of the Regat and the Zionists of the new territories joined forces in 1936 to form the Central Council of Romanian Jews with the dual aim of combatting antisemitism and preparing for emigration. As a consequence, an agreement was negotiated in 1938 whereby 50,000 Jews would be allowed to leave the country each year. Romania, with the encouragement of its Government, thereby quickly became a major centre of illegal emigration to Palestine. Although this activity helped to strengthen the Zionist movement, it regrettably could only contribute marginally to the solution of the 'Jewish problem' in Romania. As in Poland, mass emigration was, given the situation not only in the Middle East but in North America and the world generally, not a viable alternative.

Poland

Of course, the epicentre of the Jewish predicament in East Central Europe, if not the whole world, was in Poland. Its Jewish population of just over 3.1 million, according to religion in 1931, was the largest in Europe outside the Soviet Union. Representing about 10 per cent of the general Polish population, it was, proportionately speaking, the largest Jewish minority in the world and about the second largest ethnic minority in the Polish state, preceded by the Ukrainians, but followed by the Byelorussians and Germans. Unlike any of the latter, it did not, however, possess a territorial base. Constituting anywhere from about a quarter to over half of the population of all the cities in Poland, it was highly urbanized, especially in the former Congress Kingdom. Still, about 23 per cent of Polish Jews lived in the countryside, with the percentage being higher in eastern Galicia and the *Kresy*.

Reflecting their urbanized character, the majority of the Jews in Poland were engaged in commerce or industry. By the census of 1931, in fact, more had jobs in the latter than in the former, reflecting in the eyes of most observers the increasing impoverishment of Polish Jewry. As has been observed earlier, however, it was in commerce and the professions that Jewish participation was most out of proportion with their actual number. Yet, the overwhelming majority of Polish Jewry was far from being well-to-do. In our terms, they would be classified as either lower middle class or proletarian. Not unexpectedly, very few Jews were found in heavy industry or mining, in contrast to the relatively larger numbers in the clothing and food industries, where they constituted about a half and a quarter, respectively, of all those in the work force. Further corresponding to what we might expect, many Polish Jews earned their livelihoods as craftsmen – shoemakers, upholsterers, tailors, joiners and even plumbers – either working for themselves or other Jews. Employment in non-Jewish firms was rare both for religious reasons and because of discrimination by both employers and employees alike. Fearing both unemployment and a downward pressure on wages, as elsewhere, non-Jewish workers in larger manufacturing concerns resisted the hiring of Jews.

The census data are also revealing as far as national affiliation of Polish Jewry is concerned, since the people of Poland were asked, in addition to their religion, their nationality. It was, thus, possible for Jews to register themselves as Jews both by religion and nationality.

As it turned out, about three-quarters of those who declared themselves to be Jewish by religion also indicated their nationality to be Jewish. Most of the 25 per cent who did not were either assimilated Jews or ultra-Orthodox and Chassidic Jews who opposed the concept of Jewish nationality for religious reasons. Not surprisingly, the figure for this latter category was significantly higher for Galicia, where about half the Jewish population registered themselves to be of Polish nationality. Linguistic affiliation was, however, another matter. About 80 per cent of Polish Jews registered Yiddish as their mother tongue, although the figure was between 40 and 12 per cent lower for Galicia, where Polish acculturation was most widespread.

Behind these statistics, obviously, lay the rich diversity of Jewish life in Poland to which we have already referred. It could not help but influence the politics of the Jewish minority as well as its relations with the new Polish state. The mere fact of course that the Jews were recognized as a nationality was not only its first but arguably its most far-reaching achievement. Although born in the wake of the collapse of the Central Powers, the groundwork for its acceptance as a legitimate claim by the Allies, without which the Polish leadership would not have accepted it, was prepared while the Germans and Austrians still held all of what was to become Poland within their grasp. The Germans, anxious to have as much support as possible for their occupation of such a large expanse of Russian territory, looked to the Jews for help. Under their aegis banned as well as new Jewish newspapers were allowed to be published and Jewish organizations were given permission to start the formation of their own school systems after a good deal of wrangling about the schools' character. Direct Jewish political activity began as well with the Zionists soon capturing centre stage, closely followed by the folkists who, while also adhering to a broad programme of cultural autonomy, rejected emigration to Palestine as a viable solution of the Jewish problem. Alarmed by the quick rise of such seemingly radical groupings, the German administration encouraged with the help of Orthodox elements in Germany the establishment of the *Aguda** in Poland, which they correctly envisaged would counterbalance the activities of the Zionists.

Even though German policy – often being in the hands of

---

* Properly *Agudat Israel*: international Orthodox Jewish organization, and later political party, founded in Germany in 1912; dedicated to the preservation of Halakhah (Jewish law) as the guiding principle in Jewish life and society.

antisemitic officers – was not as consistently pro-Jewish as at first sight appeared, it did have the effect of not only encouraging political activity within the Jewish community, but also of spurring Jewish contact with less antisemitic elements amongst the Poles. Generally referred to as the 'activists', together with the Jews they welcomed the Central Powers' proclamation in 1916 of an 'independent' Poland with as yet undefined boundaries. For a while it looked as if the Germans' policy was about to bear fruit, but their hesitation to let the Poles exercise their right of national self-determination, as well as the revolution in Russia and the detachment of territory claimed by the Poles to the Ukraine, led to the resolution of the Polish question coming increasingly to hinge on the decisions of the Western Allies. The collapse of the Tsarist regime having strengthened his position, the leader of the antisemitic National Democrats, Dmowski, established a 'Polish National Committee' in Switzerland. Within a matter of months it moved to Paris and became *de facto* the official Polish representative with the Allied Governments.

Alarmed at Dmowski's success with the Allies, the Jewish leadership in the West sought to accommodate themselves to the situation. With the help of the British Government, the 'Anglo-Jewish Committee' even attempted to arrange a conference in a neutral country between Jewish and Polish leaders, but in the end, much to the consternation of the British, they withdrew their support for the idea because of Dmowski's antisemitism. The British-Jewish group, in fact, had already in 1915 met with two progressive Polish politicians close to the 'activist' cause who were at pains to dispel fears that there was no alternative to the National Democrats.

Even an attempt in the United States to achieve a Polish-Jewish rapprochement using the good offices of the Polish pianist and supporter of the National Committee Ignacy Paderewski failed. In April 1918 at a meeting in New York with three leaders of the American Jewish Committee, including its Chairman Louis Marshall, he claimed that if the Jews abandoned what he described as their 'attitude of decided hostility' towards Poland and supported Polish territorial ambitions (which by this time included the incorporation into the Polish state of extensive areas where the majority of the population was Ukrainian, Byelorussian or Lithuanian), Polish-Jewish relations would rapidly improve. No doubt, Paderewski and other like-minded Poles were thinking along similar lines to Masaryk and the Czechs, who valued the support they had received for their cause from Jewish circles in the United

States. The only trouble was that Dmowski and his colleagues in Paris were not willing to go along with Paderewski, who by the summer of 1918 had worked out a plan whereby the National Committee would issue a declaration in favour of Jewish equality and civil rights. His original draft was so watered-down, however, that it became unacceptable to the American-Jewish leadership. A series of meetings was held with Dmowski himself, but these proved equally unproductive. Although eventually agreeing to condemn the anti-Jewish boycotts which were under way in Poland in return for a Jewish declaration calling on the Jews in Poland to support Polish national aims, Dmowski and even Paderewski in an uncharacteristic outburst still clung to the notion that the Jews themselves were responsible for the boycott and the other manifestations of hatred they encountered from the Polish population. As a consequence, the Jewish leaders came away from the talks more convinced than ever that some sort of special treaty provision was necessary to protect Jewish rights in Poland.

Meanwhile in Poland events on the ground, as it were, changed the situation rapidly. In the wake of the defeat of the Central Powers the 'Government' they had placed in authority collapsed and Polish troops under General Józef Pitsudski occupied much of the country. Although at first assuming dictatorial powers, the former commander of the Polish legions under Austrian command, anxious to dispel Allied fears that he was pro-German, agreed to the formation of a coalition Government under the premiership of Paderewski. If there was one aspect of policy on which the followers of Pitsudski, Dmowski and the others who comprised the coalition agreed, it was in their opposition to Jewish demands for national autonomy. On the other hand, there was far from unanimity in the Jewish camp. The *Aguda* as well as the Folkists who resented the sudden ascendancy of the Zionists, and the *Bund* (the Jewish working-class movement of the Russian Pale), at this point still hedging its bets on the imminence of world revolution, also rejected the autonomist programme. As the most well-organized and most politically coherent faction, the Zionists were able to call a conference of Jewish organizations in December 1918 at which time a Provisional Jewish Council was established. Participating in elections for the Constituent Assembly which took place in late January 1919, the Council captured six of the eleven seats won by Jews. Their victory took on added significance in the light of the fact that three of the other five successful Jewish candidates were also supporters of the right of Jews to be recognized as a national group. Success, nevertheless, continued to elude the autonomists, since the only concession the Sejm (the Polish parliament) was willing to make was to grant autonomy to the local religious communes, a move designed to drive a wedge between the Orthodox and other Jewish elements.

Events in parliament soon took precedence over those in the country, especially along the eastern frontiers where the Polish authorities had to face the difficult task of maintaining their rule over large expanses of territory with, to one extent or another, hostile majority populations. In these circumstances the Jews found it exceedingly difficult to maintain even a semblance of neutrality, which hardly made them popular with either the Poles or the local Lithuanian, Ukrainian or Byelorussian populations. Additionally, there was the dislocation and privation caused by the war and its immediate aftermath. Anti-Jewish violence occurred in eastern Galicia, the worst being in Lwów (Lemberg) after its capture by Polish troops on 22 November 1919. The catalyst for the outrage in which at least 72 Jews were killed and 300 injured was the Polish commander's proclamation accusing the local Jewish population of treason. The same officer, one might add, also took measures to deprive Jews of the civil service posts they had held under the Austrians.

Similar attacks took place in other Byelorussian and Ukrainian areas, the worst of which was in Pinsk on 5th April 1919 after all those attending a Zionist meeting were arrested on the orders of the local Polish military commander. In the end, 35 people, including women and children, were murdered by firing squad. More casualties were only prevented by the quick intervention of the local representative of the American Jewish Joint Distribution Committee (known as the 'Joint') who got in touch immediately with the authorities in Warsaw. Outrages also occurred after Polish troops entered the towns of Lublin, Lida, Wilno and a number of other towns. Protests were soon heard as well from Western Europe and the United States. The British Foreign Secretary, Balfour, even took the unusual step of writing a note to Paderewski calling on his Government to take all necessary steps to protect the Jews. The Polish premier replied that his Government had, indeed, done everything it could to prevent violence, which he blamed for the most part on internal and external provocation.

Other Polish leaders responded even more harshly. Antisemitic groups, while consistently denying their involvement, blamed the Jews themselves for the violence. Similar views were even voiced by moderate and Socialist politicians, such as the prominent Polish Socialist Party (PPS) deputy Ignacy Daszynski, who placed the blame for the unrest at the feet of Austrian 'marauders' and claimed that they were 'directed against speculation'. On the other hand, there were those in the Polish community who did take a stance against antisemitism. The PPS-dominated Council of Workers' Delegates in Warsaw condemned the pogroms, asserting that they were the work of reactionary elements. Similar views were voiced by such prominent individuals as the politician Leo Bilinski, General Alexander Babianski, Professor Baudoin de Courtenay and the writer Andrzei Strug, who decried the 'conspiracy of silence' about the pogroms in government circles and the press.

A further rise in anti-Jewish sentiment was noted after the signing by Poland in late June 1919 of the Minorities Treaty, which Poles generally regarded as an infringement of Polish sovereignty and a potential tool in the hands of those opposed to the post-war settlement. Polish political leaders preferred to blame the Jews for the treaty rather than accept that it had been occasioned in large measure by their own behaviour, including their inability to face up to the scourge of antisemitism. In this regard their attitude has to be contrasted with that of the Czechoslovak Government, under Masaryk and Benes, which was consistently at pains to keep the lid on anti-Jewish violence, lest it be used as justification by the Allies to impose on them the same provisions for the protection of minorities as had been imposed on the Poles.

In the event, the situation on Poland's eastern frontier remained uneasy. Open conflict with the Soviet Union resumed in the second half of 1919, culminating in the Polish attempt to gain control of the Ukraine from the Soviets in April 1920. Anti-Jewish violence accompanied the Polish offensive and involved in particular the National Democratic troops of General Haller as well as the notorious Ukrainian forces of Generals Semyon Petlyura and Balak-Balakhovitch. With the beginning of the Soviet counter-offensive which brought the Red Army to the outskirts of Warsaw and led to the establishment of a Bolshevik-led Provisional Revolutionary Committee for Poland in which several Jews played a prominent part, public opinion, incited by unscrupulous propagandists who made a point of connecting the Jewish and Bolshevik threats, yet again directed its wrath against the Jews. Not surprisingly, the Polish retreat was thus accompanied by pogrom-like disturbances in Minsk, Siedlce, Luków, Wtódawa and Bialystok, and all along the front Jews were executed after being convicted by summary courts martial for alleged spying activities on behalf of the Soviets.

An opportunity for the establishment of better relations between Poles and Jews came with the fall in December 1919 of the Paderewski Government and its replacement with one headed by Leopold Skulski. The dominant figure in the new regime was again General Pitsudski, who felt strongly that Poland's maltreatment of the Jews had done serious harm to her position *vis-à-vis* the Allies. As a consequence, the Skulski Government, even before it took power, established connections intended to build a bridge to the Jewish leadership, which proved difficult initially because of its diverse nature. By March 1920, however, a Jewish Interparty Committee was established and agreed that its first priority should be for the Polish Government to take concerted and immediate action against anti-Jewish violence and agitation. It also demanded the lifting of all administrative and cultural restrictions which still applied to Jews. The Committee was especially adamant about the law passed in December 1919 which made Sunday a compulsory day of rest in Poland. Theoretically intended to force Jews to observe the Christian sabbath in addition to their own, it was for the most part evaded by bribery.

Except for a promise to put an end to the violence and to establish a Council for Jewish Questions, the meetings with Skulski bore little fruit. A breakthrough would have to wait for the Government of Wladyslaw Grabski, perhaps the only major figure in the National Democratic leadership sincerely interested in coming to a working arrangement with his country's Jewish population. After several successful meetings of the newly-created Council for Jewish Questions, a government crisis occasioned by the Red Army's threat to Warsaw intervened. The Grabski Government fell and was replaced by an all-party coalition headed by Wincenty Witos, a man whose openly hostile views concerning Jews made the creation of a framework for resolving the problems between Poles and Jews virtually unthinkable. The new Defence Minister, who was a close confidant of Pitsudski, did give assurances to Jewish representatives that orders had been given to the Army to stop the attacks against Jews, although he had to admit his relative powerlessness in view of the general high level of antisemitic feeling prevalent in Poland, including in the military. Over the infamous General Haller, he felt that he had absolutely no control whatsoever. Amongst the Jewish leadership bitter disappointment set in. Matters became worse during the defence of Warsaw. As luck would have it General Haller took charge of the volunteer forces which were mustered to aid the regular troops. Jewish volunteers were segregated from other units and confined to their barracks under guard. After the Soviets were repelled General Sosnowski, the Defence Minister, had Jewish officers and soldiers arrested and placed in a detention centre near Warsaw where they were guarded by avidly antisemitic troops from western Poland. At the front, anti-Jewish excesses accompanied the advance of Polish troops. Not surprisingly, even worse than the Poles were their allies, the Ukrainian legions of Balak-Balakhovitch and Petlyura. Wherever Jews were found to have participated in the pro-Soviet Polish Revolutionary Committee reprisals followed against the Jewish population as a whole.

With the easing of the military situation in the East a return to normalcy followed. Protests from left-wing and liberal circles even led to the release of the Jewish soldiers being held at the infamous Jablonna detention centre, although some twenty of the detainees were killed in a suspicious railway accident near Lublin while returning to their homes.

With the end of the Russo-Polish war calm was finally established in Poland. Antisemitic violence continued, but on a much smaller scale. The years 1918–20, as far as the Jews were concerned, could not be forgotten. In their eyes the new Polish state became the embodiment of antisemitism. Relations between Poles and Jews had reached the point at which a meeting of the ways was made difficult, if not impossible. They were not given much hope by the attitude and policies of the Government once peace was restored either. In line with the National Democratic crusade against the Jews, they were, despite the existence of an ostensibly democratic constitution, virtually excluded from the civil service, the officer corps of the army and the teaching profession. Although an attempt to institute a *numerus clausus* had been defeated in 1923, Jews found it exceedingly difficult to obtain places at the country's universities. Government contracts were awarded to Jews only in exceptional cases, and the legislation of 1919 prohibiting work on Sundays remained in effect.

It should not come as a surprise, therefore, that the Jews of Poland welcomed the coup d'état of 1925 which brought back to power General Józef Pitsudski. A former Socialist and bitter opponent of the National Democrats, he was by Polish standards a moderate nationalist who shunned antisemitism as a political or economic weapon. Although his ten years of rule were characterized by the participation of Jews in government and the absence of official antisemitism, a fundamental change in the nature of Polish-Jewish relations failed to take place. While theoretically a federalist, Pitsudski showed no more inclination to give the Jews a measure of autonomy than he did to the Ukrainians or the Byelorussians. Jewish cultural institutions continued to be denied public funding and for Jews economic discrimination remained a fact of daily life. One is tempted to observe that as long as the political consensus continued to be influenced by the popular hatred of Jews, there would be little room for change. The period following the war had shown, moreover, that this hatred had a depth and intensity which could easily become transformed into political action as well as popular violence against Jews.

If Jewish efforts to achieve autonomy in the political realm were for a variety of reasons not successful, the same could not be said of those in the cultural sphere. Within a short space of time there was a flowering of secular Jewish cultural life unlike any experienced before or since. Based on Yiddish, it had its roots in the pre-war period. Yet it was born in the unique circumstances of independent Poland, which had united into one state the Jewries of the Congress Kingdom and Galicia with those of the Eastern borderlands, thereby creating a Jewish minority with the linguistic as well as demographic prerequisites for an independent culture.

A host of daily and weekly newspapers came into existence, the two most important being *Haynt* and *Moment* published in Warsaw. The Yiddish theatre flourished, as did literature, allowing such talented writers as Y Y Trunk (1887–1957), Olizer Varshavsky (1898–1944), and I J Singer (1893–1944) to have their work published and taken seriously by a wide readership. The younger brother of the latter and Nobel laureate, Isaac Bashevis Singer (b.1904), who made his literary debut before he left Poland for the United States, has often spoken about the uniquely productive atmosphere of this milieu.

This flourishing of Yiddish culture extended, as well, into the fields of education and scholarship. It gave birth in 1921 to the Central Jewish School Organization (or *Tsisho* as it was known after its Yiddish initials) which, despite constant wrangling between the various factions of *Bundists*, Zionists, Folkists and even Communists, achieved modest success in enrolling by 1934–35 some 15,000 pupils in its network of independently-funded primary and secondary schools. Besides offering instruction in the Yiddish language, they were intended to promote a national diaspora-oriented, secular Jewish culture. As one would expect, the largest

number of Tsisho schools were in the *Kresy*, while there were none
in Galicia, where not only was acculturation most prevalent and
state education the accepted norm, but also Orthodox and
Chassidic elements most entrenched in their opposition to the
secular programme of the Yiddishists. Amongst secularly oriented
Jewish parents, on the other hand, there was a general reluctance
to allow their children to be educated in anything but the majority
language of the country. Even if they supported the Jewish parties
at election time, read Yiddish newspapers and books, attended the
Yiddish theatre and spoke Yiddish in their families and amongst
their friends, they took the understandable view that entrusting
their children's fate to the Yiddish school system had the potential
for placing unnecessary barriers to their participation in society as a
whole later in life. In the final analysis, then, despite its high quality
the Yiddish school system, in being able only to draw a small
proportion of the total number of Jewish schoolchildren in Poland,
was a failure.

The picture with Hebrew culture in Poland was just the reverse.
In the education sphere the *Tarbut* (in Hebrew, 'culture') school
system, backed by the moderate Zionists, established a network of
primary and secondary schools in which Hebrew was taught as a
living language and used as the language of instruction for all
subjects, except Polish language and history. Over time, as
conditions in Poland worsened and more Jews looked towards *aliyah*
as a way out of their plight, the enrolments at the *Tarbut* schools
increased, so that by the mid-1930s they were attended by some
37,000 Jewish schoolchildren. This figure becomes all the more
impressive when one realizes that there were also other Zionist
schools in Poland – the *Yavne* of the Mizrahi, the *Braude* secondary
schools and the *Schul-kit* system of the right wing of Poale Zion. As
with the *Tsisho* schools, they were primarily a phenomenon of the
Kresy. In Galicia and the former Congress Kingdom they had to
fight a losing battle against both the Chassidim and acculturation.

Despite the inroads of the Zionists and Yiddishists, Jewish
education in Poland continued to be dominated by traditional
elements. Sponsored by the *Aguda*, the Khoyrev schools for the boys
and the Beys Jakov schools for girls by 1934–35 claimed over twice
as many pupils (110,000) as the *Tarbut* and *Tsisho* school systems
combined (50,000).

When all was said and done, however, the fact remained that the
majority of Jewish children in Poland, about 60 per cent, were still
enrolled in state schools. Not only was the historic trend in Galicia

and the former Congress Kingdom towards Polish acculturation difficult to counter, but for most secularly oriented Jewish parents an education either in Hebrew or in Yiddish seemed to place unnecessary constraints on their children's progress in a society that was already inhospitable enough.

The fundamental volatility of the situation of the Jewish minority in Poland was tested by the onset of the Great Depression, which hit Poland with particular intensity. Predictably, anti-Jewish feeling began to increase significantly, although as long as Pitsudski was alive it remained, so to speak, politically inert. As fate would have it, then, his death, in May 1935, came at the worst possible moment for the Jews. In the ensuing struggle for power between the Pitsudski loyalists and the newly-reconstituted National Democrats, known as the National Party, egged on by its radical off-shoot, the National Radical Group, the Jewish question could not help but become a major issue.

The ruling camp of National Unity excluded Jews from membership and sanctioned a programme of economic self-sufficiency which the then Prime Minister defined as an 'economic struggle [against the Jews] by all means – but without force.' One of the main aspects of this policy, which had the full support of the Polish Catholic Church, became the encouragement of Jewish emigration. Thus the Polish Government intervened on behalf of the Zionist cause with the British and favoured the ill-fated Madagascar plan of 1936. Only the PPS, the Socialists, remained steadfast in their opposition to antisemitism, although even in their ranks there were those who saw emigration as the only possible solution to the Jewish question.

Encouraged by the success of the Nazis and the antisemitic right elsewhere, the National Democrats and their allies pursued their campaign against the Jews both inside and outside parliament with unremitting intensity. In 1936, a law, modelled on legislation introduced by the Nazis in Germany, severely limiting ritual slaughter by Jews was passed, while at the universities Jewish students were terrorized and segregated. 'Aryan paragraphs' were adopted by a number of professional organizations. Worst of all, government-supported economic boycotts of Jewish businesses were organized, which at times deteriorated into pogrom-like excesses. It has been estimated that in 1935–36 alone, some 1,399 Jews were wounded and several hundred killed in antisemitic attacks in over 150 Polish towns and villages.

Ultimately much worse than the pogroms was the impact of the boycotts on the economic well-being of Polish Jewry, which was already suffering under the effect of the depression and encouragement of 'native' Polish (i.e. non-Jewish) business activity. By the late 1930s, as stated earlier, one in three Polish Jewish families was reliant on outside assistance (mostly from the American 'Joint') to keep itself above the poverty line.

While some of the resulting despair manifested itself in an increase in suicides and apathy amongst Jews, a good deal of it also became translated into a turn towards extremism in the political arena. It led within the Zionist Movement not only to a strengthening of the Revisionists and the Socialists, to some extent at the expense of the General Zionists, but also to an increase in the numbers of persons, mostly young people, who were emigrating or preparing to emigrate to Palestine. Just as significantly, it led to a broadening of the appeal of the *Bund*, which by the late 1930s as a consequence of its victories in various local and national elections emerged from the Jewish working-class movement to become arguably the single most powerful Jewish organization in Poland. A good number of Jews, in the working class as well as the intelligentsia, turned to the secular left, both the PPS and the illegal Communist Party, for a solution to the Jewish problem.

In the last analysis, then, not even the crisis of the 1930s had managed to make the political unity of Polish Jewry any less elusive than it had been in the 1920s. In a sense, the fronts hardened and became more fluid at the same time. Increasing numbers of Polish Jews, especially amongst the young, may have for example turned to Zionism, but the movement became so deeply divided into opposing factions that it could hardly be called a single movement any longer. However much the *Bund* had been able to broaden its base of support, especially in Warsaw, the *Aguda*, let alone more extreme traditional elements, remained an intransigent and entrenched minority who would never make common cause with either the Zionists or the *Bundists*. Lastly, although there may have been some movement between the latter two groups, an alliance between them would have been virtually inconceivable, since the one group fervently believed that the solution to the Jewish problem lay in the advent of socialism in Poland and the other believed just as vehemently that the Jews' only hope lay in emigration to a Jewish National Home in Palestine. It could be argued that the achievement of unity amongst the Jews would not have had much of an effect on the way in which they were treated in Poland anyway, since the determining factor was increasing Polish antisemitism under the impact of a deepening economic crisis. There was simply no way the Jews of Poland, even if they had formed a unified bloc, could have had much influence on a situation that was effectively beyond their control.

Ultimately, of course, the fate of Polish Jewry did not even rest in the hands of the Poles, but in those of the German invaders who together with the Soviets dismembered Poland in 1939. At first, for about the first six months of the occupation, the Germans were satisfied to isolate the Jews from the Poles. They were expelled from the countryside and forced to move to the cities where they were subjected to special regulations and treatment. To prevent Poles from helping Jews evade this policy decrees were introduced severely punishing those who did, and a constant barrage of Polish specially designed antisemitic propaganda was kept up to prevent the Poles from developing any sympathies for the Jews. A reign of terror began in which thousands of Jews were killed at random and most of the synagogues were destroyed. The Germans also inducted many Jews into forced labour. Whatever their fate later on, 300,000 or so Jews managed to escape the Nazi grip by fleeing to Soviet-occupied territory.

Having gathered the Jews in the cities, the Germans proceeded to ghettoize them. First came Lódz in May 1940 and finally Warsaw in November 1941. The ghettoes thereby created were administered by Jewish bodies which were successors to the Jewish Councils (Judenräte) set up when the occupation began under the close supervision of the German authorities. The same procedure was followed with the former Galician territories captured from the Soviets. By the end of 1941 the process of ghettoization was completed. Now, the Jews were completely isolated from the rest of the Polish population. Their already meagre rations were further reduced and forced labour became the norm. As a consequence, in this period about 500,000 Jews died of disease.

For the Germans this was not enough. At the end of 1941 they implemented the third and final stage of their war against the Jews. In December the first deportations began from the Wartheland to the newly-established death camp at Chelmo. Next came the liquidation of Lublin ghetto at Belzec, followed by the first series of deportations from Warsaw and the removal of the Jews of Kraków to the nearby killing centre at Auschwitz. Soon afterwards, in April 1943, the SS returned to complete the liquidation of Warsaw where they encountered the largest scale armed resistance by Jews in the Holocaust. Small arms were no match, however, for tanks and

artillery, and within less than a month the ghetto was liquidated.
Within a few months, Lwów and Lódz were also cleansed of Jews,
the last 70,000 being deported from the latter in August 1943. The
remaining Jews in Poland were either in slave labour (the Germans
intended to kill them as soon as they were replaced by Poles) or in
hiding, either with resistance groups, with individual Polish families
or 'on the Aryan side' with forged identity papers. At the end of the
war, some 50,000 to 70,000 Jews were found to have survived – in
hiding (thanks mostly to courageous help from non-Jewish Poles),
in the Polish Army or concentration and forced labour camps in
Germany. A further 150,000 were eventually repatriated from the
Soviet Union. In the end, some 3,000,000 Polish Jews had perished
in the Holocaust, the greatest number killed in death camps on their
own soil. These sorrowful statistics speak for themselves: the long
history of Polish Jewry had come to an end. Whatever came
afterwards must be regarded as a postscript.

Territorial changes resulting from the Second World War
Antony Polonsky: The Little Dictators (Routledge & Kegan Paul)

The Post-war Years

Yet, especially in Poland, events showed that the 'Jewish question' did not entirely 'resolve itself' with the murder of the vast majority of the country's Jews. Pogrom-like excesses greeted the Jews returning to their homes after the war, the most notorious being in Kielce, where 42 Jews were killed and many more injured. For this and other reasons as well, many of the Jewish 'returnees' chose to emigrate, mostly to Israel, rather than remain in Poland. Of those who stayed, a small but significant number assumed key functions in the Russian-installed Communist regime of Poland, a circumstance which did not endear them to those sections of the Polish population which fell victim to the Stalinist excesses and purges of the 1950s.

It can be said, in fact, that not just in Poland, but throughout the East Central European region in the post-war period, it seemed as if Jews could not help but do the wrong thing. It started with their return, whether from concentration camp, hiding, exile or the army. As we have seen, antisemitism in the region was far from being an exclusive German import. A good many people were glad to see the Jews removed from their midst. Some even reaped material benefit from the removal of their Jewish neighbours by acquiring their property, their jobs or their clientele. Thus, it came to pass that Jews returning to their former homes were greeted with varying degrees of indifference, hostility or, as in Poland, even violence. Not surprisingly, many Jewish returnees chose emigration to North America, Palestine or elsewhere rather than endure hostility and harassment in the lands of their birth.

In the meantime, Soviet-style regimes were installed throughout the region and, as a consequence, for the first time in history Jews entered positions of leadership and influence in government, industry, education and the arts. However, as the late British historian Hugh Seton-Watson observed as early as 1945,

> it is doubtful whether the young nations of Eastern Europe, whatever their political, economic, and social regime, will for long tolerate in the most prominent places of their economic and intellectual life people whom they cannot help regarding as strangers.

Moreover, especially as the behaviour of the new Communist regimes became more excessive, the Jews were identified with a system that was becoming increasingly unpopular. To quote the knowledgeable observer of the Eastern European scene Paul Lendvai:

> *Jews were now prime ministers and secretary generals, ministers and police chiefs in the same countries where their fathers and relatives had been barely tolerated aliens and where only a few years earlier they had been deported or killed amid the general indifference of the population. The people now hated and despised them even more intensely than they had their ancestors.*

Non-Communist Jews fared no better than their Bolshevik cousins. As members of the former middle class they had not only had their property expropriated but faced persecution, harassment, discrimination and surveillance from the government as well as the jealous resentment of the population at large, who often felt that they received their just deserts.

With certain local variations this was the pattern which defined the relations between the Jews of East Central Europe and their non-Jewish neighbours in the post-war period. As far as the practice of the Jewish religion was concerned, the policies of all the governments of the Communist bloc – of which Czechoslovakia, Hungary, Poland and Romania formed a part – were governed by the Marxist-Leninist opposition to all religion *per se*. There were some differences, however. It was first of all easier to suppress the official practice of Judaism than the dominant religion of the region, Roman Catholicism, which also had the backing of the Vatican and millions upon millions of loyal adherents throughout the world. All the same, especially early on, the Czechoslovak and Hungarian regimes were even successful at suppressing the practice of Roman Catholicism, not to mention Protestantism.

Hungary and Romania, which today have the largest Jewish populations of the region, represent exceptions to this pattern. Although as elsewhere Jewish religious and cultural life has been tightly controlled, it has been allowed to continue in these two states on a scale unimaginable in Poland or Czechoslovakia, let alone in the Soviet Union. Budapest, today, still boasts the only rabbinical seminary in the Eastern bloc and in Romania there is still a Jewish school system. Romania, moreover, was the only Warsaw-Pact state to maintain diplomatic relations with Israel after the Six-Day War.

Furthermore, as already indicated, not only did a great many, if not most of the Jews remaining in Poland, Czechoslovakia, Hungary, and Romania tend to be secularized to the point of being non-practising, but the many of their number who were Communist Party members were often amongst the most ardent opponents of all religious practice whatsoever.

After Stalin's decision to withdraw the Soviet bloc's support for the State of Israel in the wake of the Korean War, the Communist regimes' suppression and control of the Jewish religion became intertwined with their campaigns against Zionism. Such Jewish after-school education as still existed was tightly controlled and restricted, as were Jewish youth groups and the other cultural activities of the Jewish communities, which in any case were by this time headed by loyal party functionaries. As still in the Soviet Union today, many individual Jews were intimidated to the point that they severed whatever ties they still had with the Jewish community.

The anti-Zionist campaign initiated by Stalin also took on another dimension. It became one of the fulcrums of the purges of the early 1950s as well as a new vehicle for antisemitism. Stalin and his stalwarts in Hungary, Poland, Romania and Czechoslovakia played upon the popular resentment of the Jews to rid their ranks of comrades who were seen to be potential opponents of the Stalinist order or who simply stood in the way of their own advancement. It did not matter whether these new enemies of the people were loyal leaders at the pinnacle of their parties, such as Slanksy in Czechoslovakia, Rajk in Hungary or Pauker in Romania, who until being deposed themselves had led the Stalinist terror against the supposed Communist and non-Communist opponents of their regimes. They were put on trial, found guilty, executed and put in prison like anybody else. It did not matter, moreover, that they had severed all their ties with Judaism and Jewry; that they were, in fact, orthodox Marxist-Leninists who unquestionably opposed all religious activity and ethnic deviation, and had obeyed the dictates of the party till the very end, often even to the point of confessing to crimes of which they were not guilty.

What made them such easy victims, scapegoats if you will, however, was the very attribute which they were at pains to deny or ignore – their Jewishness. It was very often the single most important reason for their being singled out in the first place and it was what made the charges against them personally as well as the purges in general seem warranted in the eyes of the population at large. Branding them as 'cosmopolitans' and 'Zionist internationalists' played upon the notion common amongst all the peoples of Eastern Europe that the Jews were a foreign element pursuing their own aims and always ready to conspire against the nations amongst whom they lived. In the notorious show trial of Rudolf Slansky and other leading Communists in Czechoslovakia the prosecution went so far as to take great pains to point out that the Jewish defendants had been raised in German-speaking homes and/or had been members of Zionist-oriented organizations in their youth.

Discrediting Communists of Jewish descent by invoking nationalist antisemitic sentiment was retained as a weapon in the hands of Stalinists and neo-Stalinists of East Central Europe into recent times. It was used by the notorious General Moczar and sanctioned by First Secretary Gomulka in the Polish antisemitic campaign of 1968 as well as later in the year by the Soviet and indigenous opponents of the 'Prague Spring' in Czechoslovakia. These later instances of officially-sanctioned antisemitism, however, for several reasons turned out to be largely counter-productive. Anti-Jewish sentiment was simply no longer as widespread, even in Poland, by the late 1960s as it was immediately after the war, and many people believed that any group which incurred the propagandist venom of the regime deserved sympathy and support rather than antipathy.

Antisemitism, of course, continued to be prevalent in anti-Communist circles, especially amongst right-wing exiles in the West. During the Hungarian Uprising of 1956, furthermore, there were a few days when popular vengeance manifested itself against Jewish functionaries and members of the Secret Police. A few years ago antisemitism raised its head as well on the right-wing fringes of the Solidarnosc movement in Poland. More recently, as we shall see, it has surfaced in the wake of Communist rule amongst right-wing elements in Hungary and Romania. Even though anti-Jewish feeling no doubt continues to exist as an undercurrent in Eastern Europe (as it does in the Soviet Union), it has simply lost its potency as a political weapon. Very few Jews by now remain in the region, and there have been serious efforts, from oppositional as well as official elements, to educate the general population against anti-Jewish prejudice. In Poland, for example, the Government has acknowledged that the Gomulka regime committed a grave injustice by supporting the antisemitic campaign of 1968 which drove most of the Jews who remained there after the war out of the country.

But Jews had been leaving Poland before 1968. The first major wave came immediately after the war and lasted until the Soviet

Union's reversal of its policy towards Israel around the time of the Korean War. Many Jews returning to their homes not only in Poland, but in Hungary, Czechoslovakia and Romania as we have already seen, voted with their feet and went on *aliyah* to Israel or emigrated to North America and elsewhere in the West. The next major exodus of Jews from Eastern Europe came from Hungary, in the wake of the failed Uprising of 1956. In the late 1950s and early 1960s, during the post-Stalinist thaw under Khrushchev, Jews were again allowed to emigrate from Poland, Czechoslovakia, and, especially, Romania. As more recently with Soviet Jewry, this emigration was achieved only after protracted negotiations and with the help of the United States as well as other Western governments. The years 1968 and 1969, in addition to the mass exodus of Jews from Poland, also saw the departure of many Jews from Czechoslovakia in the wake of the Soviet invasion of August 1968 which brought an end to the 'Prague Spring'.

Interestingly, as a consequence of the Holocaust and the territorial changes both before and after the war, there was even some Jewish migration within the region itself. A fair number of Slovak Jews fled to Hungary, especially Budapest, during the war in the hope that under the Horthy regime they would be better able to escape persecution and deportation. Some of those who survived remained in Hungary after the liberation. Then there were Jews from Sub-Carpathian Ruthenia who like their co-religionists from Slovakia had survived in the Hungarian capital, or had made their way to Hungarian territory after their former Czechoslovak province had been ceded to the Soviet Union in 1945. Some Sub-Carpathian Jews also made their way westward into Czechoslovakia and some, of course, remained in Soviet territory. By the same token, there were also Jews from those Romanian and Polish territories which were incorporated into the Soviet Union who managed to 're-settle' in Romania or Poland, respectively.

The efforts of numerous individuals notwithstanding, Jewish life in East Central Europe is but a shadow of its former self. With the murder of so many millions of Jews in the Nazi death camps and the emigration and religious persecution as well as the territorial re-distribution of the post-war era, the situation could hardly be different. Significant numbers of Jews nevertheless continue to live in the region, and, as we shall see, there are growing signs that the current trend towards democratic pluralism is taking hold in Poland, Hungary and Czechoslovakia. Despite continuing political instability, it seems likely that the same will even happen in

Romania. The only cloud on the horizon, except of course the faint possibility of a wave of reaction in the wake of a fall from power in the Soviet Union of Gorbachev, is the spectre of the revival of antisemitism, which might again flourish in the unsettled political and economic conditions currently developing in Eastern Europe.

Personal Memoirs

Hugo Gryn

Stephen Roth

Ben Helfgott

Hermy Jankel

Memories of Czechoslovakia: Hugo Gryn

Hugo Gryn is the senior Rabbi of the West London Synagogue, and as such is a leading figure in the British Jewish community. More than that, he is well known outside of Anglo-Jewry. He frequently appears on the radio and television and is recognised as one of the foremost exponents of Judaism in the media. He was at one time Rabbi of the Jewish community in India and has served in the United States.

He was born in Czechoslovakia, a country to which he returns from time to time – although, as the following story indicates, his actual nationality and the languages he spoke became somewhat confused.

At the age of 13, he and his family were taken to Auschwitz. His younger brother vanished the day they arrived at the camp, never to be seen again. He and his father stayed together throughout their time there, although his father died of typhus shortly after liberation. His mother, although separated throughout the time they were at Auschwitz, survived and returned to Czechoslovakia where she subsequently died many years after the war.

Hugo Gryn came to Britain early in 1946. After learning English, he studied at universities in Cambridge, London and Cincinnati and was ordained rabbi at the Hebrew Union College in Cincinnati.

Hugo Gryn today

Hugo Gryn: Cemeteries. That is what I think of when I think of the land of my birth, Czechoslovakia.

Always a lot of nostalgia, but the image that perpetually comes to mind is the cemetery in Prague. Partly because some of my own direct ancestors were buried there – a very evocative, beautiful cemetery, if there can be such a thing. But also, more than anything else, it sums up for me what that country means for my generation.

That cemetery in Prague, in the middle of the city surrounded by all that goes on, close to a very beautiful river, baroque buildings – and some modern ones, too – is symbolic.

The cemetery itself dates from the sixteenth century – with some tombs containing 12 or 13 people buried one on top of the other; they were so anxious to make it last. All chock-a-block with tombstones bearing the most wonderful inscriptions and symbols.

That is the image because, although life goes on, for people like me, it only speaks about the past. There is no future. It is very much my own past as well.

The old cemetery in Prague. Hugo Gryn finds he *has* to keep going back there. It contains the remains of his distant ancestor the famous Rabbi Loew.
Judy Goldhill

Remembering. Rabbi Hugo Gryn at the memorial to the citizens of his home town Berehovo (Hung: Beregszász) in the cemetery at Holon in Israel.
June 1986.

Being a descendant of the famous Rabbi Loew – he of the well-known Golem story – whose grave is in that cemetery, I feel doubly conscious of that fact. Always I place my own little stone on that tomb of his, and there is a similar attraction for my own children.

Not very far away in Karlovy Vary, which used to be Karlsbad, is my mother's tomb and both are closely connected for me. They are the only monuments that I have of my family. One is a very remote one, from centuries ago. The other my own mother's. For the rest of my family, there are no *matzevot* (monuments) – anywhere.

So the personal attachment is very close. But also, the fact that in that cemetery there are those masses of tombstones huddled together – almost surrealistic, the way they lean in and lean out, some are cracked and some you can hardly read – creates a special mood.

I am particularly moved by them when I visit in the winter. The greyness everywhere, sometimes a little snow. They only speak about the past. But they have very little to say about the present or the future.

From that cemetery, one visits the vestiges of Jewish life still remaining – the community centre close by, the Altneushul dating back to the thirteenth century, the Kosher restaurant. Mostly full of old people. People, you can't help thinking, who are waiting to join the others in the cemetery.

But then surprises – among the old people are some young ones, who are in the process of returning to Judaism, to a consciously Jewish life. Not many of them. But they are there and so I am not prepared to write off the community, although, objectively, I see no future for them.

So different from the memories of the Czechoslovakia of my early boyhood. All my memories are of Jewish life there, interrupted by the events that preceded the Holocaust. We in Czechoslovakia had inklings of what was going to happen before the Second World War began. Mr Chamberlain's 'piece of paper' had an intense effect

The Gryn family before the holocaust destroyed it. Left, his mother, Bella, who survived the camps and died in 1964 at Karlovy Vary (Karlsbad); Hugo; his younger brother Gabriel, who died in Auschwitz; and his father Geza who died in Mauthausen, May 1945.

on my life and on that of all the other Jews in what he called that 'far-off land'.

My home was in a part of Czechoslovakia that became Hungary and is now in Russia. In those days, the area was made up of Czechs – and even among them there were Moravians and Bohemians and Sudeten Germans – and Slovaks. The only Czechoslovaks were the Jews. We were great patriots.

We had a Czech flag. And we also had a Jewish flag. In the Czechoslovak Republic you could be Jewish by nationality – and there was a very good reason for that. Czechoslovakia was put together by the great powers in 1918. It hadn't existed as an independent country before then.

Its population contained a proportion of Hungarians, quite a lot of people who were Ukrainians, and then there were the Jews. It was the most democratic country in that part of Europe and was to last only 20 years.

In those 20 years, they wanted to show that this was truly a pluralist society – an experiment *à la* Switzerland.

Had they gone only by linguistic distinctions, my part of the country would probably have been Hungarian. That the Czechs did not want and so they allowed the Jews to opt for Jewish nationality. This meant several privileges – among them to have our own schools. So I went to the Jewish school.

It was a primary school where the languages of instruction were Czech and modern Hebrew. In our own home we had three languages. There was Hungarian, there was German – that was the *elegant* language and I think my family wanted to be elegant. And then there was Czech – because we wanted to be patriots.

Much later – long after the war when I was living in the United States – the question came up: what was my mother tongue?

On a visit to Karlovy Vary, I asked my mother the same question. She stopped and looked at me – blushed, I think – and said, 'I don't remember either . . . It has to be one of three.'

Strangely, the one language we didn't have in our home was Yiddish, although my grandparents were Yiddish speakers and I was to learn Yiddish in later life.

So the earliest memories are school, the Jewish community – which was really an all-embracing one – and a tremendous sense of optimism, born I suppose of the success of my father. He was mainly in the business of forestry developing and timber – one of the really well-known Jewish occupations. I never had any pocket money, yet I never remember wanting for anything.

My mother was trained in medicine but never practised. She married well, and that was that. We had her notes and some of her books around, but whenever anything was wrong with either my brother or me, we went to a proper doctor – a woman who studied together with my mother and they were very close friends.

I don't think it is just nostalgia. But life had a very beautiful rhythm to it.

Religion was in the air we breathed, so we were a religious family. The Jewish calendar determined the shape of our life. For instance, you wore winter clothes until Passover, when the spring clothes came out. It could be still freezing, but it was *Pesach* so we put on spring clothes.

With *Succot*, the autumn harvest festival, winter clothes came out again. It could be quite hot, but that's how the calendar worked.

Likewise, our diet. From *Succot* onwards, the *Shabbat* lunch was always *cholent*, that mixture of meat, beans, barley and dumplings which kept you as warm within as your clothes kept you warm without – a dish prepared the day before so as not to infringe the

The Neolog Synagogue in Kojmary Street, Zilina.
Jan Weill, Beth Hatefutsoth

When a group of ultra-Orthodox Chassidim moved into Berehovo, they were given the name Neolog (Reform). This is a Neolog rabbi, Dr Hugo Stranski, speaking at a memorial ceremony at the Zilina cemetery for Jewish soldiers killed in World War One.
Jan Weill, Beth Hatefutsoth

Sabbath prohibition about cooking on Saturdays. But it tasted wonderful even to those who weren't religious. After *Pesach*, that came to an end because it wasn't a summer or spring dish.

Always for *Pesach* there were new clothes – and to this day I cannot celebrate *Pesach* without some new garment, maybe even just a pair of socks or a new shirt. But something new, there has to be.

Shabbat – the best way I can describe it is the analogy with Jerusalem. Whenever I am in Jerusalem over the Sabbath I always think of my home town, Beregszász (in Hungarian – or Berehovo in Czech or Beregovo in Russian – it probably had other names, too, but these are the only ones I remember).

On Friday afternoons, our town just wound down – just as Jerusalem does. The town had a population of about 25,000 and 15,000 were Jews. As far as I can remember, every shop was Jewish-owned, except for one non-Jew who had a tobacconist's kiosk. So every Friday afternoon, all the shops closed – and remained so until *Havdalah* time on Saturday, when the Sabbath ended. In winter time, when this was quite early, the shops opened again on Saturday evening. Sunday was market day.

It was natural that everybody went to the synagogue on *Shabbat*. This was a real community. There were a number of synagogues, and all but one of them belonged to the community.

The community was, of course, Orthodox.

The one synagogue that didn't belong to the community was the 'Reform' congregation – because when they came to the town, mainly from Poland and various points further east, they decided that the local community was not strict enough for them. They had their own *mikveh* (ritual bath houses), their own Talmud Torah schools and I believe their own *shechita* (kosher animal slaughter).

Because they weren't part of the community, they had to have a special Act of Parliament passed in order to benefit from certain state subsidies.

Some time in the late 1920s, they went to see the member of parliament for our town – a Jew who belonged to one of the Neolog synagogues in Prague.

This man put through the required Bills, but there was one problem: what would it be called? I guess he was something of a missionary – and suggested that they should call themselves the 'Berehovo Neolog Congregation'. The Chassidim had no idea what this meant, and agreed. So you had a situation in which the synagogue to which the ultra-Orthodox Jews in town went proclaimed over the archway to its courtyard or *hof*, 'Berehovo Reform Congregation'.

When the weather was fine, the whole community, it seemed, went out on one of the walks around the town that were particularly popular. There were lovely mountains in the area and my own family had a vineyard. It became a prosperous business for my father.

You would see all your family and friends walking the same way. It was most idyllic.

Relations with the few non-Jews around were practically non-existent, as far as I remember. I can't think of any socialising with them at all.

Everything, of course, changed with the Munich agreement and the dismantling of Czechoslovakia.

In many ways at this time, we were the more fortunate Czech Jews. Our town was not part of the territory ceded to Germany; it went to Hungary. But Hungary was part of the Nazi bloc – it was to be an ally of Germany in the war – and almost immediately, we started to feel the effects of what that meant: to suffer antisemitism.

I became aware of it even before the country ceased to exist, and in a most horrible way.

My father's parents lived in a village about 15 miles away. As a seven or eight year old I was quite adventurous and used to cycle there. This was Vary, a village with a sizeable Jewish population, too.

I used to have to go through two or three other villages to get there, a place situated in a triangle where two rivers merged – the river Borzsa and the river Tisza. One side of the Tisza was Czechoslovakia where Vary was situated. The other side was Hungary.

One of the big 'industries' in this village was horse smuggling. Somehow the price of horses was never the same on both sides of the river. Wherever the price of horses was higher, that was where they were taken – usually at night and on rafts.

I have to say that one of the few skills I really have to this day is horse smuggling. You wrapped their hooves in lots of heavy sacking and you put over their heads a well-filled bag of oats and, believe me, those horses were silent all the way across the river.

November 1938 was when we officially became Hungarians. About three or four weeks before, early one morning, we were awakened by a phone call from an uncle of mine – a younger brother of my father – in Vary. He was very, very agitated.

'Come at once,' he said. My father left immediately and asked me if I wanted to come, too. I said, yes.

Young as I was, I thought my father needed some kind of support.

We drove there at great speed. And there I saw a scene that has been with me ever since.

During the night, some Hungarian terrorists – a word that was as appropriate then as it is now – had crossed the river with only one purpose: to terrorise the Jews.

My grandfather was the local rabbi or *rav* – but he was also, in the historic Jewish tradition, a farmer.

He kept cows – cows that now had been butchered in the most gruesome way. Their bellies had literally been torn open. And I saw that. It has stayed with me ever since – to the point where if I could draw, I'd draw that scene now perfectly from memory.

That was my first encounter with antisemitism.

Therefore, when in early November the Hungarians came into our town I had, even then, the worst forebodings. I was only eight, but I remember very, very clearly how I felt.

It was an orderly withdrawal of what remained of a Czech administration – a few troops – and their replacement by Hungarian divisions, lots of Hungarian flags being waved. I cried while everyone else was full of excitement. I started crying when the Czechs left and I continued to cry when the Hungarians came in – even though they were accompanied by bands and guns and horses and all the things that are supposed to excite a young boy. In the light of what happened a little later on, so much of what accompanied that procession was just pathetic.

The Rabbi of our town, Solomon Hirsch, a lovely man of great dignity with a fine voice, and a friend of the family, had been an officer in the Austro-Hungarian army during the First World War.

Now, for this occasion, he dressed up in his army uniform – and there he was together with the other dignitaries of the town to receive the people coming in. He wore his decorations, too.

Also there, similarly dressed, was an uncle of mine, my mother's elder brother. Lots of Jews dug out their uniforms and did the same thing.

I don't know what they thought they were doing. Perhaps they genuinely believed this was the right way to carry on. I was not old enough at the time to comprehend it.

But I have often thought of that scene and of the betrayal that was to come. Not long afterwards, the antisemitic laws followed.

For me, it became terribly obvious, because I had to change schools.

The best school in town was the gymnasium – the academic

high school. This gymnasium declared a *numerus clausus*. In a town that was at least 50 per cent Jewish, it was decided that not more than 3 per cent of the school membership could be Jewish.

I had to take an entrance examination – and then passed. I became one of the three out of the hundred that were admitted. My family was delighted. But if one could be depressed at that age, I was in the midst of a deep depression. I did not wish to be one of a percentage. The interview I had was very unpleasant. The people who conducted that interview were Hungarian officials who had been imported to do that job. I was so miserable that my father took pity and started to phone around looking for another school for me.

He found a Jewish gymnasium which had boarding facilities in Hungary itself – in the town of Debrecen.

I loved my school – a very fine school indeed with some marvellous teachers; men who had been sacked from the universities and other establishments of higher learning and could only find jobs in Jewish schools. Because this was one of the finest Jewish schools, we had some of the best teachers.

One of the treats we used to have was to go to film performances on Sunday mornings at the local cinema – hired specially for the boys in the two boarding houses at the school because we were considered to be too young to go to the evening performances. It was a treat and we saw a complete programme of whatever was being played that week, including the newsreels.

At this time, something sinister was happening, which became only partly apparent from watching those newsreels, but which affected the people back home.

Carpathia was split in two now, part of it Hungarian and part run by Ukrainian Fascists, who simply drove the Jews out. Where could they go? Some moved into our town – including members of our family.

My parents had to rent a couple of houses to accommodate them. That was in 1939.

Many of these newcomers were from Poland. In addition, there were a number of people in the town who were not officially of Hungarian nationality, whose parents could not prove they had Hungarian antecedents. Never mind that they were born in Berehovo. These, the Hungarians decided, should not be allowed to stay in Hungary or what was deemed by them to be Hungary. They were ordered to be deported. Except that they used a kinder term – 'resettlement'.

Our own papers were found to be in order.

Meanwhile I was at school in Debrecen and watching a newsreel. There on the screen we saw how the glorious Hungarian troops were beating the hell out of the Russians.

I found myself watching not the guns and the troops which were supposed to gain one's attention and enthusiastic support but the civilians in the background, trudging down the muddy, rain-swept roads. I could recognise them. They were people from my home town; families that I knew – carrying suitcases and moving, clearly, towards the front where their destiny – as cannon fodder – was to suit the Hungarians very well.

School regulations decreed that we had to write a weekly letter home. That afternoon, I wrote mine – and described in great detail to my parents exactly what I had seen.

That, I think, was the first news that came to our town of what

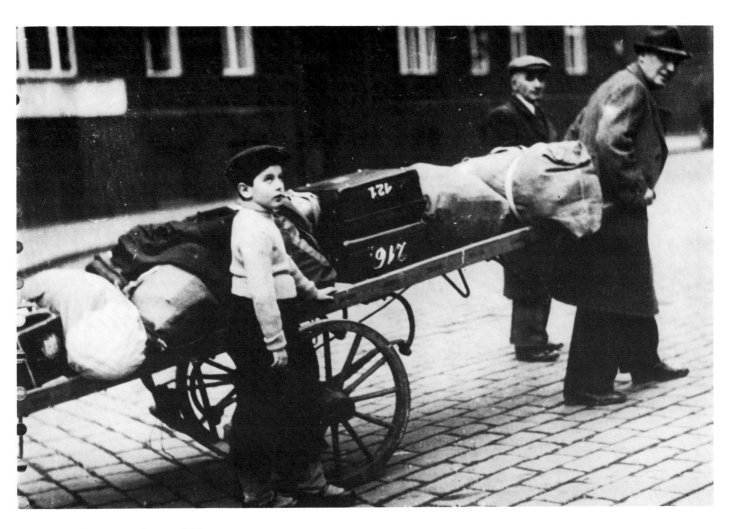

They called it 'resettlement'. For the Jews of Czechoslovakia it was holocaust.
Wiener Library

had happened to our friends and families and what that dubious term 'resettlement' really meant.

The men of military age from our town had by then been recruited – not as soldiers, of course, but as back-up labour battalions. It was forced labour, from which almost none returned. They were the ones put in the firing line.

They were really doing the same thing to us children. Throughout the state school system, schoolboys were required to have military and paramilitary training. This presented a few problems to the authorities as far as we Jewish school boys were concerned.

We also had to go out one afternoon a week to do something for the war effort. What could they do to us? They gave us shovels and made us juvenile labour battalions. It wasn't difficult to see the absurdity of all this.

It was all designed to humiliate us. We had to stand alternately to attention or at ease – with those idiotic shovels.

Usually, we were taken to the local gasworks where our job was simply to move one pile of coke from one place and put it down in another place. It was totally unproductive work and we knew how much time we were wasting.

Our teachers had to do it, too.

While we loved the school, we knew that we were marked by going there. We had a badge on our caps that said very clearly we were from the Debrecen Jewish Gymnasium.

Nearby, was a Lutheran school – and always there were fights between us. Eighteen-year-olds would beat up eleven-year-olds.

But there was an ironical twist of fate in all this. Our gym instructor was Karoly Karpati – who just happened to have won a gold medal for Hungary in the 1936 Berlin Olympics – for wrestling.

Mr Karpati taught us self-defence – how to deal with street fights. One of the things he taught me was not to be afraid in a street fight. I had some street fights and realised that he was right, one of the important things was not to be scared. I was beaten up a few times, but I tried not to be frightened.

When the Gestapo moved in in 1944, things became a lot more sinister.

Up till then our family had had some trouble. My father had been arrested and interned. But there was bribery and corruption and he managed to buy himself out. It was easy to see that this was a means of fleecing the Jews of what they had. There would be other, harder exercises.

Just before *Pesach* 1944, I came home from school, travelling by train. At a place called Csap, a couple of cars were added to the train. They were filled with SS soldiers, in their black uniforms with the death's head insignia on their caps. The cars were uncoupled – at Berehovo. When I got off the train, so did the SS.

What they did in our town was precisely planned and devilishly clever. The Germans had already done their intelligence work and knew they were arriving at a place with a very large Jewish population.

They knew who they would find there when they arrived. For one of the first things they did was to arrange for the immediate arrest of about 30 leading members of the community, every one of whom had been carefully hand-picked. They were either the popular leaders of the community or the heads of large families.

The trek to deportation starting with a railway station in Moravia, under the eyes of Nazi soldiers. A clandestine photograph taken in January 1943 by Jan Pavelcic.
Wiener Library

The Germans announced that they were being taken as hostages – and would be released unharmed if they were ransomed.

The sum they set was in the local currency – an enormous amount – a million pengo. If the money came by eight o'clock, the men would be released. If the money didn't arrive, the hostages would be shot.

There was an immediate collection in the community.

Already, I knew my way around officialese and I was part of the collecting team – carrying a soap box in which money would be dropped by these frightened citizens of Berehovo.

By mid-afternoon, it became quite clear that nothing like a million pengo could possibly be raised. In the whole town there wasn't that sort of money.

So the leadership – and that included my father, who was not among the hostages – went to the Gestapo headquarters and told them they couldn't raise more than perhaps half.

The Nazis thought and then came to a conclusion. They didn't want to fight with the Jews, they said. They wanted to work with them. So they would extend the deadline by twelve hours and would take, at fair valuation, jewellery and certain categories of bank books.

The collection began again.

Whenever I read in the Torah that bizarre scene where the Children of Israel make the Golden Calf after collecting jewels from the women, I think of those scenes in our town. For that is exactly what happened. Women gave their jewels, their gold bracelets, necklaces, whatever they had. The deadline was extended again and then, sometime during the night, the Nazis decided they had the equivalent of the million-pengo ransom they had been demanding.

They released the hostages.

My thoughts were not clear then. But years afterwards I realised that this was the point when we had walked into the trap. The insidious nature of it all had been carefully worked out.

First of all, we Jews in the town were entirely cashless. We no longer even had the price of a railway ticket. But there was an even more sinister result.

We had concluded we could 'trust' the Germans as people who kept their word. They had promised to release our people in exchange for a million pengo. When we handed over the money, the people were released. Therefore when the time would come for further 'resettlement', everybody involved would believe it. And so it turned out.

We were all running scared. For a time, we managed with food. It was an agricultural area and people hoarded food.

And then other things started to happen.

First of all, they announced that all the Jews would be segregated into a ghetto – just outside the town in an area covered by a very large brick factory, large sheds and a couple of saw mills, one of which belonged to my father and his partner.

The Jews had to leave their homes – one suitcase per person, all very carefully prescribed – and were then taken there.

Food was brought in from outside.

Hugo Gryn with his mother Bella at Karlovy Vary in December 1945, months after being released from the camps.

Then hundreds of neighbouring villages were emptied of Jews who were also brought in. The overcrowding was terrible.

Some of the intelligentsia in the town committed suicide including one of our family doctors, Dr Hubert. I saw him carted out.

You had the feeling that the Hungarians were delighted. There were now these empty houses, with carpets, pictures, fittings and so on, just waiting to be looted and taken over.

The Jews, meanwhile, were oblivious to their fate. When they were told they would be resettled in the East to do agricultural work, they believed it. If they had thought that any other fate awaited them, there is no way anyone would have boarded that train.

To give one some idea of how well the Nazis' 'night and fog' programme worked, when the transports started from the ghetto – daily trains, sometimes two a day – I watched carefully and saw how orderly it all was.

While the transports were proceeding, I behaved as I frequently did – I was nosy. I noticed a slip of paper stuck to the side of one of the wagons. It bore the route that the train would be taking. I took it to my father and our friends. Nothing sinister was read into it.

It had our town as the start, then went on to list the others we would be passing – a place in Slovakia, Presov, then Cracow. And finally a place we had never heard of. It was called Auschwitz.

Memories of Hungary: Stephen Roth

Stephen Roth, unlike the other participants in this book, was active in the Zionist movement throughout the entire Holocaust period – working in the heart of Budapest.

He came to Britain after the war, where he established himself as a leading figure in the Anglo-Jewish community. He has been Director of the Institute of Jewish Affairs in London and Chairman of the Zionist Federation of Great Britain and Ireland. He is also a prominent member of the Board of Deputies of British Jews. At present, he is Chairman of the European Zionist Council.

Stephen Roth today.
John R Rifkin

Stephen J Roth: It was over 20 years before I returned to Hungary from the time I left in 1946. The decision to return was made easier by going as a member of a delegation of the World Jewish Congress, led by its then President, Dr Nahum Goldmann, to the Jewish community of Hungary. I am not sure I would have gone on my own; if I had done, I would have been more absorbed in personal reminiscences than I was on this official visit, with all its business engagements, when one is somewhat cushioned against sentimentalism.

As a member of a delegation to the Jewish community, I naturally had many an opportunity to observe Jewish life and contrast it with previous times. Nobody knows for sure how many Jews there are in Hungary today – and 'today' could just as well be 1967 as 1990 because there has been hardly any Jewish emigration from the country during the last 20-odd years. The last big 'bloodletting' took place in 1956, during the Hungarian uprising. At the time, 20,000 Jews left the country among an estimated total of 200,000 émigrés. There is, however, a natural demographic decline, owing to the unfavourable age structure of the survivors of the Holocaust and on account of mixed marriages. Present estimates vary between 80,000 and 100,000, of whom at least 80 per cent live in Budapest. The number of those registered with the communities is, of course, small. The true figures have to be estimated on the basis of the few occasions when non-registered Jews suddenly reveal their identity: the Yom Kippur service, particularly the prayer for the dead, when the synagogues are packed to overflowing; the sale of matzot at Passover; and, to a certain extent, the funerals. While some claim that the 'official estimates' given by the community are somewhat inflated for the purpose of obtaining social and cultural benefits from abroad, others believe that there are in fact many more Jews but that they are so assimilated and distanced from their Jewish identity that they cannot easily be detected, let alone quantified. Either theory may be valid. But I noticed within a few days the interesting phenomenon that, while there were a great number of mixed marriages amongst the young, social contact among older generations remains confined largely to Jews. Some of these older Jews will have nothing to do with the Jewish community but their friends and bridge partners remain Jews.

Visitors from abroad are invariably impressed by the degree of Jewish life which still exists in Hungary. And so they should be, if Jewish life there is compared with the position in other East European countries (except perhaps Romania), or if one considers that, with all the genuine facilities for the exercise of religious freedom, in its political philosophy and educational policies the regime has been basically inimical to religion and particularistic identities. But for me, who knew the pulsating pre-war life of 200,000 Jews in Budapest and 400,000 in the country at large (during the Second World War, with the re-annexation of some of the territories lost in the Trianon Peace Treaty of 1920 to Czechoslovakia, Romania and Yugoslavia, the number increased to 725,000), the overwhelming impression was not of how much there was in the way of Jewish institutions but of how little remained. Yes, there is a rabbinical seminary, the only one in Eastern and even Central Europe; but this institution, which was once one of the great centres of Jewish learning, now has only ten or twelve students. Yes, there is still a Jewish secondary school (gymnasium), named after Anne Frank, but it is the last institution of this kind and a small one in a country which, before the Second World War, had 11 Jewish secondary schools, 144 elementary schools and two teacher-training institutions. Yes, there is a Jewish hospital in Budapest, but it is not the old one which had 670 beds and 14,000 patients per year, one of the country's best hospitals which was, rightly, the pride of Hungarian Jewry; only a former small subsidiary hospital could be preserved. I could go on like this through every aspect of Jewish life. The institutions which are understandably admired by other visitors appeared to me as but shadows of the past – the few walls which have not crumbled in the great catastrophe.

It should be emphasised, however, that this tragic decline in Jewish life was mostly the product of the Nazi era and the annihilation of 600,000 of the then 725,000 Jews in Hungary. The Communist regime must be complimented for maintaining and supporting what exists. At the same time, however, the negative Communist approach to religion which permeated the post-war period inevitably lessened further the demand for Jewish facilities.

The structure of the Jewish community also provides a strong contrast with the past. Before the war there was a plethora of Jewish organisations in Hungary. After the war, the Government united them all in one overall organisation. Even the religious differences between the minority Orthodox and the so-called Neologs – the majority trend which, by its outlook and customs, roughly corresponds to the more traditional wing of the US Conservatives – did not justify, in the eyes of the authorities, the existence of two bodies; but the Government made the concession of permitting a semi-autonomous Orthodox section to operate within the unified community. A further sign of discontinuity – and a startling difference from Jewish life in the West – was that voluntarism in communal life had completely disappeared. This was perhaps inevitable in a system in which people did not have the means to afford and the spare time to do honorific work. Most of the leaders were full-time officials of the community and, consequently, a tendency towards bureaucratism had replaced voluntaristic communitarism. Its worst effect was that even the few people who would take an interest in serving the community had no opportunity for involvement. This added to the depletion of the ranks.

My home town

The picture becomes much more sombre when one goes out to the provinces. I lived in Budapest practically from the age of 18, when I went up to the university. The years of my childhood and youth were spent in my birthplace, Gyoengyoes, a small town of 20,000 inhabitants, 100 kilometres north-east of Budapest where I would also return later for holidays and vacations. About 10 per cent of the population was Jewish. This small community of 2,000 Jews maintained two congregations, an Orthodox one of some 500 souls, to which my family belonged, and a larger one of the more reformed trend. Both had their synagogues, Talmud Torahs and other institutions, and Jewish life was active and flourishing. This was, incidentally, the pattern in every other provincial community.

Naturally I went to visit my home town, if for no other reason than to visit my father's grave. Only some 20 Jews are left. With the utmost difficulty do they maintain the semblance of a community. The only institution worth mentioning is the cemetery with its impressive memorial for the town's Holocaust martyrs. But most of the tombstones are neglected, overgrown, or half sunk into the earth. Nobody looks after them except lone visitors like myself, turning up occasionally from far away.

I know practically every house in Gyoengyoes. I had known all the Jewish inhabitants. As I walk in the familiar and yet so strange streets, memories come back. Here lived my schoolmate who perished in the forced labour battalion into which Jews were conscripted. There lived my parents' friends, deported to Auschwitz. Over there is the house of my sister's best friend, who miraculously survived and now lives in Canada. And so it goes on, from house to house. I pass the building of the high school where I matriculated; of

The young Stephen (originally Siegfried) Roth – aged three watched over by his elder brother and sister

the ten Jewish boys in my class, only three survived. Gyoengyoes has grown remarkably and is now a busy city. But, to me, these Jewless houses and streets looked frighteningly empty. It was not a silent emptiness; it cried out with a shrill pain which pierced my heart and brain.

Distance helps to refine memories. My childhood was on the whole a very happy one, sheltered by a harmonious and closely knit family, with wonderful parents and a brother and two sisters to whom I have remained very attached all my life. But, looking back after so many years, not just with the hindsight of an adult but also with the traumatic lessons of the Holocaust and the new experiences gained from living in the more advanced West, I suddenly realise that, as a Jew, my life in this small Hungarian provincial town had been one of abject degradation. I go to visit the house in which I spent my childhood; how often did little street urchins shout after me in this street 'Dirty Jew!' – probably without knowing what they were saying, just repeating what they had heard from their elders. I never had a single gentile friend nor did I ever court a non-Jewish girl. My parents' social contact was only with Jews; the club where my father went daily after lunch for a coffee and a *shmuz* was officially called the Businessmen's Club but, in fact,

Above:
Moritz Roth, father of Stephen, outside the family's home in Gyoengyoes.

Right:
Stephen Roth at the time of his barmitzvah – with his grandfather and two sisters in the courtyard of the house at Gyoengyoes.

was frequented exclusively by Jews, with the sole exception of the town's mayor who went to play cards with 'his Jews', partly for sound electoral reasons but also because he had a special liking for Jews. In the state gymnasium in which I was educated, most of our teachers were known to be antisemites (but I have to add, in fairness, that, although they occasionally made antisemitic remarks, in their professional work they treated the Jewish pupils absolutely correctly). The sports club of the town did not admit Jewish members, and as an act of courage and defiance the Jews established their own sports club which, again euphemistically, was named Gyoengyoes Businessmen's Sports Club. One of the most vivid experiences of my boyhood, which helped to shape my outlook on my Jewishness – I could call it my first Zionist experience – was when, by the luck of the draw, the football team of this 'Jewish' sports club had to play against the larger local club of the non-Jews. The supporters of that club did not this time cheer their team with the usual encouragement 'Forward Gyak!' (which was the name of the club) but 'Forward Hungarians!' In no clearer way could *vox populi* have indicated that we Jews were just thinly tolerated aliens.

Actually, for me, that experience was not even a shock. It was

The garden of Roths' summer home near Gyoengyoes in 1932.

Stephen Roth aged 18. A school photograph taken at the time of his 'Matura', when he finished high school.

merely a confirmation and crystallisation of what I had always felt instinctively, because of the education by my parents and the pattern of our life: we were Jews, not Magyars, and, being an alien minority, we had to put up with certain inequities. The young generation of Jews today, born after the Holocaust and after the emergence of the State of Israel, particularly those in tolerant Western countries, may find it difficult to understand this but, in our powerlessness, we lived reconciled to the fact that *der Jid is in Goles*, the Jew lives in exile.

Within this limitation, and by 'knowing one's place' among the majority population of the country, one could be reasonably happy. We lived on the margin of society but within a satisfying society of our own. And, in purely material terms, Jews could do very well. At the same time, we were enriched in our Jewish environment by the best of Hungarian culture – a culture which I still admire for its splendid literature and artistic creation, and which is not sufficiently appreciated abroad because of the language barrier.

All these memories came back to me, clearer than ever, when I walked the streets of Gyoengyoes 20 years after my departure and 23 years after the destruction of Hungarian Jewry. Making, as I tried to do, an intellectual rather than an emotional assessment, the destruction of the Jewish community did not look so unbelievable. We should really have foreseen it, although the brutality with which it was carried out would have been inconceivable even to the worst prophets of doom. We failed to understand the full meaning of *goles*. But on one point my views have not changed, even if the younger Jews of today cannot understand it: there was little we could have done about it – other than to go away. Well-to-do and influential as many individual Jews may have been, there was no such thing as 'Jewish power'. It was the realisation of this which made me a Zionist in my early youth, at a time when Zionism was championed only by a small minority and was highly unpopular within the great masses of Hungarian Jewry.

Hungarian Jews were opposed to Zionism because they hoped that somehow they could achieve equality with other Hungarian citizens, not just in law but in fact, and that they could be integrated into the country as Hungarian Israelites. The word 'Israelite' denoted only religious affiliation and was free from the ethnic or national connotation attached to the word 'Jew', which they therefore regarded almost as a derogatory term. Hungarian Jews did attain remarkable achievements in industry, in culture, some even in politics. But even the most successful Jew was not accepted by the majority of the Magyars as one of them – as the Hungarian reaction to the Nazi invasion of the country has so tragically demonstrated.

The years in Budapest

University days were not very different. Jewish students kept together, ostracised by almost all the others. Every autumn, at the beginning of the academic year, there were student demonstrations organised by the right-wing unions, when the Jews were at best thrown out of the university building or frequently cruelly insulted and beaten up. But by that time I really did not concern myself with the motive and reason; I only revolted against the rudeness and crudeness with which my Magyar colleagues expressed their non-acceptance of the Jew.

I was active both in the general Jewish student union and even more in the Zionist body, *Maccabeah*, as well as in the Zionist youth movement at large. I pitied my non-Zionist colleagues, with whom we Zionists were engaged in all-night debates, who simply could not cope with the antisemitism around them. They desperately tried to be 'accepted' or to disappear among the non-Jews, often Magyarising their names for that purpose, and developed an ideology of Hungarian-Israelite patriotism. Some joined the lamentably weak liberal, democratic or social-democratic parties which, in the reactionary Hungary of the day, with its anti-democratic system of open elections, had no chance of success. Others found an answer in joining the equally weak and illegal Communist Party. (One of my most interesting debating partners from the Communist side, with whom I developed a feeling of mutual respect and friendship, became a national hero in Hungary for his resistance work under the

Roth was heavily involved in the work of the Zionist Underground. Here, in 1943 aged 28, with three Polish refugees who, with him, were leaders of the Hanoar Hatzioni movement.

Nazis, and had streets and cinemas named after him and a stamp with his picture produced in his honour.)

The Zionist point of view was not helped by the official Hungarian approach to minorities. Having lost two-thirds of its territory after the First World War because of the minority population, Hungary did not recognise and, indeed, resented minorities in the period between the two world wars. This also determined its attitude to the Jews. Whereas in all surrounding countries – Czechoslovakia, Poland, Romania and Yugoslavia – Jews were recognised as a national minority, with Jewish nationality declared in the censuses, Jewish parties in parliaments, etc., in Hungary Jews were recognised and accepted only as a religious group. This was a completely hypocritical approach which suited the Hungarians, and the Jews tried to benefit from it and endeavoured to convince themselves that it was, in fact, the truth.

This attitude has persisted into the post-war era, in spite of the fact that in the Soviet Union Jews are recognised as a nationality *de iure* and in some of the other East European countries *de facto*. But while the USSR provided a model in many other areas, in its approach to religion, minorities and similar matters Hungary followed its own sovereign way, more determined by history and tradition than by Communist ideology or the Soviet example. The absence of an ethnic recognition of Jewry had its advantages: it is probably the reason why in Hungary – in contrast with Poland, Czechoslovakia and Romania – no *Jevsekcia* emerged to take over the running of the Jewish community. If being Jewish is only a matter of religion, as the official Hungarian theory had it, it was difficult for the Communist Party, with its atheist philosophy, to have a Jewish section.

However, the purely religious character of Jewish life also had its disadvantages. For a long time it seems to have inhibited the Jewish community from engaging in cultural work of a secular character, for instance in arranging courses in Jewish history, literature or art, lest this were to be regarded as a national or nationalistic activity. It obviously would have required a special effort to explain to non-Jews that, in the case of a national religion like Judaism, the national elements cannot be divorced from religion. However, while this problem seemed to be very relevant at the time of my first visit, in subsequent years I found gradual improvement in this respect and cultural activities are now, in fact, quite considerable.

At the time of my university studies, Hitler already ruled in Germany and the shadow of Nazism was soon felt also in Hungary.

A medley of Nazi parties sprang up which, to show off their separate Hungarian identity, adopted a number of variations of the swastika: the Scythe Cross, the Clubbed Cross and the most infamous Arrow Cross. The worst, however, was the Hungarian appeasement of the Nazis by the introduction, from the spring of 1938 onwards, of a series of anti-Jewish laws restricting the role of Jews in economic and cultural life and engendering mass dismissals and the mass unemployment of Jews. Already the first of these laws excluded me from my chosen career: to practise as a lawyer.

Soon a stream of Jewish refugees came from the neighbouring Nazi-occupied countries to Hungary – first, from Austria, then from Slovakia and Croatia, the two Nazi-created puppet states, and later from Poland. Most of them came illegally and, when detected, were put into internment camps. The 'official' Jewish community organs avoided any contact with the 'illegals', as such contacts would fall foul of Hungarian law. But they set up a large social network which, among other things, assisted those who were interned or who, through their discovery by the police, became 'non-clandestine'. It was left to the small Zionist movement and some Orthodox groups to assist the 'illegal' refugees with funds, false papers, accommodation and in every other way. The Zionists went even further than assisting the arrivals: they organised the sending of emissaries into Slovakia and Poland to seek out Jews and smuggle them into Hungary.

During these years my own activities were entirely devoted to this refugee work. I was a member of the *Vaadat Ezra v'Hazala* (Aid and Rescue Committee), established at the initiative of Jerusalem, and, because I spoke German very well (which was the nearest to Yiddish), I was among the few who could communicate with the escapees from Poland. (Through my daily contact with them I ultimately picked up Yiddish, a language most Hungarian Jews did not speak at home.)

Hungary was then an island in the Nazi ocean. Although restricted or deprived of livelihood, and although most young Jews were forced into the labour service, where some 40,000 perished, the Jews lived in relative freedom. We felt that we had the task not only of rescuing as many Jews as possible from neighbouring countries but also of chronicling events. In 1943 I was asked by the community leadership to establish with two other colleagues a small institute where we assembled documentary material and took numerous eyewitness testimonies from refugees. It was my first essay in contemporary Jewish research.

Hungarian Holocaust

But ultimately Hungary shared the fate of the other European countries. On 19 March 1944 the Germans marched in. The Zionist leadership and its Aid and Rescue Committee immediately set up a sophisticated network of underground rescue operations. One of its functions was the smuggling of Jews across the border: instead of bringing them into Hungary as we had done until then, we now smuggled them out into safer Romania. I was one of the people in charge of this operation. But, first, on the very day of the occupation, I had to burn the entire archive of our small research institute.

After some three months' clandestine activity, one of the small groups I had tried to send over to Romania was caught at the border and, no doubt by torture, the Gestapo got my name out of one of the members. I was arrested in Budapest, taken to the Gestapo headquarters for 36 hours' uninterrupted interrogation – which

Raoul Wallenberg's heroic work on behalf of the Jews of Hungary is well known. He not only made representations for them, he also recorded what was happening. This is his photograph of Jewish women on their way to deportation – being marched through Budapest to a holding camp, prior to their 'transport'.
Beit Lohamei Haghetaot

meant 36 hours' uninterrupted beating – and finally thrown into the Gestapo prison in one of the main Hungarian prisons taken over by the Germans for this purpose. I had a few more interrogations and, three months later, was assigned with 100 other prisoners to a transport to Auschwitz 'with special designation' which, in the Nazi camouflage language, meant 'without selection' (i.e. straight into the gas ovens). The story of the miraculous escape of this transport through the intervention of Admiral Horthy, who was still Head of State and whom we succeeded in alarming through a letter smuggled out of prison, is too complex to be related here. All that should be said is that I experienced having the death sentence pronounced over me, wrote and smuggled out my farewell letter to my family and, ever since, have felt as if I have been given the gift of life a second time.

Out of prison and after a few weeks in a Hungarian internment camp I returned to the Zionist underground. While I was imprisoned, the movement had organised itself under the cover of the Swiss Embassy. This peculiar arrangement was based on the fact that the British mandatory authorities in Palestine had made 7,800 certificates available to Jews in Hungary. Switzerland was the representative of Britain, and the Hungarian authorities agreed that possessors of foreign immigration visas could receive a foreign 'protective passport' until emigration. This device was actually invented by Sweden (which later took a more active part in the rescue of Hungarian Jews through the mission of Raoul Wallenberg) but was made maximum use of by the Zionist underground under the Swiss flag. Its activists became 'Swiss Embassy officials' who not only issued the permitted number of 7,800 protective passports but forged their own documents ten times over.

One of the Zionist supporters was a plate glass merchant who, as an advertisement for his wares, built a glass house (a rarity at that time and the only one in Budapest). He made this house available as a Swiss Embassy branch office dealing with the 'representation of foreign interests'. A glass house was a most unsuitable building in the midst of the daily bombing raids, but it was the only one we had. When the Arrow Cross came to power on 15 October 1944, and the turn of Budapest Jewry for deportation arrived (the provincial Jews had all been deported by July), the Zionist 'Swiss officials', with their families, moved into the exterritorial safety of the glass house. As the knot tightened, more and more people were brought in, until it became an asylum for some 3,000 people who literally slept on steps and in corridors, under the most appalling alimentary and sanitary conditions. This was our life for some three months, until liberation by the Russians on 18 January 1945.

It was a peculiar feeling to visit these places – the prison in the Foe-utca, the glasshouse in the Vadász-utca. It all seemed so far away – not at twenty but hundreds of years' distance. I felt no hatred, no desire for revenge, just a strong feeling of how right I had been to emigrate soon after the war.

I have been back to Hungary many times since 1967. Every year I see colossal progress. The political liberalisation, the market economy, with its private sector in which many Jews found profitable occupation, the willingness to accept foreign investments, have all led to a tremendous rise in the standard of living (however low by Western standards) and to a pleasant improvement in the lifestyle of the city. Actually, I like Budapest today, with the exceptional beauty of the reconstructed castle on the hill overlooking the Danube, its excellent cultural institutions,

Jews wearing yellow stars lining up for deportation, under the guns of Hungarian troops.

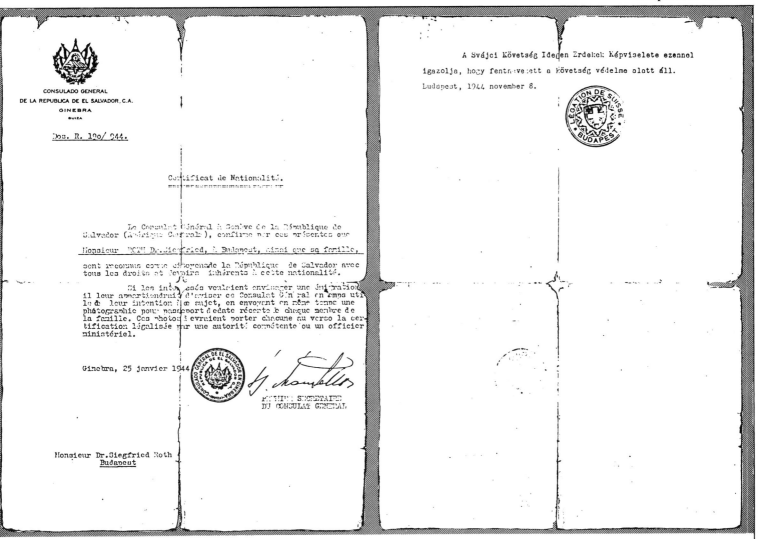

A certificate sent from the El Salvador Consulate in Geneva showing that Stephen (né Siegfried) Roth had become a citizen of El Salvador and confirmation from the Swiss Embassy of extending protection to Roth as a foreign citizen.

museums, opera, theatres, its civilised hotels and good restaurants (I am told that even the nightclubs are first rate) and with much of its old Bohemian spirit and wit having survived. But beyond these outward appearances which make Budapest a favourite tourist city, there are deeper values to be appreciated. I like the spirit of openness with which people, even those who are party members, have been willing to discuss political and social problems, with a healthy self-criticism of their own indoctrination, even before the change from monolithic party rule to an open democratic society.

One of the most startling changes I found during my subsequent visits, even during the last years of the gradually liberalised Communist regime, was in relation to the Jewish question. In 1967, when I went back for the first time, it was still taboo. If anything was written about antisemitism or the Holocaust at all, it was presented as being the sole responsibility of the Germans, with the Hungarians portrayed as mere victims or, at best, innocent bystanders. In the last fifteen years or so, a few non-Jewish writers, historians and sociologists have begun a daring search for the truth.

They have started to face the Hungarians' role in the Holocaust, their responsibility in the massacre of their Jews and the antisemitism which preceded and facilitated it. In other words, they are engaged in an attempt to come to terms with the past. This work has been undertaken with commendable frankness, culminating in a series of initiatives taken in 1984, on the occasion of the fortieth anniversary of the deportation of Hungarian Jewry. It has led to contacts with Jewish historians abroad, including in Israel, to the publication of books and the production of films on the Holocaust, and includes the setting up, by the Hungarian Academy of Sciences, of a team in its Institute of History to write the history of Hungarian Jewry. There is still antisemitism and there are still antisemites; but not at governmental or administrative levels. Hungary has also been pleasantly subdued in the chorus of East European anti-Zionist propaganda.

There are also positive developments inside the Jewish community. Young people discover and take an interest in their Jewishness. The first rallying point was the Friday night service and *kiddush* at the Rabbinical Seminary, to which many were attracted by the charismatic figure of the recently deceased Professor Alexander Scheiber. Fortunately, these Friday night gatherings have survived him. The Jewish Museum has been reconstructed by the Government. The Bible has recently been republished in Hungarian. Jewish educational materials and programmes for children of various age groups have been prepared on Jewish history, holidays and customs. An exhibition on Hungarian Jewish history, prepared by the Beth Hatefutsoth in Tel Aviv, received governmental permission to be shown in Hungary.

These were the first signs of greater freedom, still under Communist rule. As the party gradually reformed itself into what they now call a Socialist Party, and opposition parties freely emerged, Jews have also taken advantage of this new liberalism. The 'centralisation' of all Jewish activities in one communal organisation is a matter of the past (though it still exists in the religious field). New organisations sprang up, most important among them a Jewish Cultural Association, formed by Jewish intellectuals, academics, writers and media people, mostly of the post-Holocaust generation. They are secularists in their outlook, emphasising Jewish culture and ethnicity, and want to have few dealings with the religious Community. Their activities are wide-spread and impressive, conducted with enthusiastic voluntarism – a sharp contrast to the previous Government-controlled organisations. The latest addition to the wave of new Jewish organisations – and politically the most interesting one – is the Hungarian Zionist Federation (with a number of youth movements already in place), revived 41 years after being banned by the Communist Government and the first Zionist body to emerge in liberalised Eastern Europe. It was perhaps the culmination of my 'Memories of Hungary' that, as Chairman of the European Zionist Council, I was privileged, at a festive inaugural meeting, to receive back into the family of European Zionism a movement which formed and educated me in my youth and of which I was once a leader.

Most decisive in the new atmosphere is the impact of Israel and world Jewry. The establishment by Hungary of relations with Israel, first on a lower and now on a full diplomatic level, has given a tremendous boost to the recognition of Jewish identity, as do the numerous Israeli visitors to Hungary and even more so, the freedom of Hungarian Jews to visit Israel, of which they make much use. Similarly, contacts with Jewish organisations abroad have developed strongly. Several, like the World Jewish Congress, the Jewish Agency and the AJDC, have established offices in Budapest and the WZO has taken some hundreds of kids to Israel to summer camps and seminars and sent *slichim* to Jewish youth camps in Hungary. The learning of Hebrew is widespread and has become something like a symbol of Jewish identification.

A most promising plan is the creation of a Jewish Day School of 12 classes (for the ages of six to 18) into which the present Anne Frank High School would be merged.

When I go to Hungary today, I no longer make the sombre comparison of 1967 with 1939. I rather compare the present with the sombre picture I saw in 1967 and this is more encouraging. The effect of the Holocaust has, of course, not disappeared. Indeed, under the new freedom antisemitism (that probably was latently present all the time) has again come to the fore – and that worries Hungarian Jews a great deal. But at least I can see a Jewish community that is engaged in a cultural and organisational revival, trying to build for itself a new Jewish life – hopefully in a democratic and pluralistic new Hungary.

April 1990

Memories of Poland:
Ben Helfgott

*Ben Helfgott, a London businessman, came to Britain in August 1945
together with a few hundred other teenage concentration camp survivors.*

*He was born in Poland, and spent his early childhood in the town of
Piotrków – 26 miles from Lódz.*

*He was British Weightlifting Champion and record-holder over a
number of years and represented Britain in the 1956 and 1960 Olympic
Games, as well as the Commonwealth Games in 1958.*

*Since then he has been involved with many Jewish organisations and
has been very active in communal affairs.*

Ben Helfgott and his wife today.

Ben Helfgott: Excitement! That is the emotion that more than any other comes over me whenever I return to Piotrków.

I look at the buildings and they are still the same as they were when I was living there. Outwardly, little has changed.

I walk on the streets that I walked as a boy – the same streets! In my mind I see those walking with me, not as they are, but images of those with whom I walked and played all those years ago.

As I walk along the pavements, I am acutely aware that it was here, on these same pavements, that my parents and youngest sister – who were all later murdered by the Nazis – went about their daily business unaware of what fate had in store for them.

I am conscious too of the close proximity to my family. I feel enveloped by their warm embrace. I know that just being there is the most tangible contact I can have with my parents, sister, members of my family and all my friends who perished so tragically.

After a time, however, I feel as if I can't get away quickly enough. I am being choked. I am suddenly overcome by a feeling of injustice. Feelings I rationalise totally when I am at home in England have a quite different meaning to me when I am back where it all started.

Then, I become overwhelmed yet again by nostalgia. Somehow my appetite to return to the ghosts is insatiable. I imagine a drug addict faced with the problems brought about by his addiction feels rather the same way. I only feel that way while I am away. Soon after I go back there, I have had enough – although I know I will be drawn back again and again.

The Helfgott and Klein families lived within a radius of 60 miles and whenever I go back to any place with which my family had connections, I have the same strong emotions.

On a recent visit to Poland, I travelled together with my sons, along a route indelibly imprinted on my memory, and visited the homes of my grandparents, uncles, aunts and cousins. Like me, my sons were overwhelmed by the experience of coming face to face with the reality of the past – such is the pull of those roots!

In September 1939, the Nazis entered Piotrków and by November 1939 we were forced to move into the Ghetto – the first to be created in Poland. In these two months, we had already learnt not to expect too much help from the local Polish population. There were however some exceptions, of whom Mr L was one. On our recent visit, my sons and I spent some time trying to contact him.

There were a couple of false starts, introduced to people who

The Helfgott family in the 1930s.

couldn't remember us at all, or wished not to do so. One man said disdainfully that he had a cousin 'who did business with the Jews'. Eventually, we found him. I remembered this man, tall, good-looking, in his early thirties.

'Do you remember Helfgott?' I asked.

Immediately his face lit up. The memories came flooding back to this man – and his recollections confirmed all that I had myself remembered. He mentioned names of people I knew in addition to those of my parents and my sisters.

I was just 13 years old when I last saw him. He didn't remember me, although he remembered my younger sister. There was good reason for him not to remember me. He had helped to hide my parents and my aunt during the deportation of the Jews from the Ghetto to the gas chambers in October 1942. I was unaware of the whereabouts of my parents and anxious to make contact with them. I broke away from my work detachment and made my way to his house. When I enquired about my parents he scolded me and said, 'What are you doing here? Don't you know how dangerous your presence is here? If the SS were to find you they'd shoot you together with us.' I pleaded for shelter but he refused. Eventually he acceded to my entreaties and asked me to come back in the evening when, under the cover of darkness, he would take me to my parents' hideout.

As I walked away, wandering aimlessly in the outskirts of the town, and absorbed in my own thoughts, I suddenly heard a cry, 'Jew!' emanating from a group of Polish boys. I wasn't sure that it was directed towards me but, frightened, I started to run and they chased after me. Fortunately, I was near the park, the landscape of which was familiar to me because I used to play hide and seek there before the war. I found a hiding place where I took refuge and stayed there until my pursuers gave up the chase.

Later that evening I returned to Mr L, who then took me to my parents' hideout. What an emotional reunion that was!

This man remembered the family extremely well but forgot me, probably because I represented an episode which he had tried desperately – and successfully – to expunge from his memory.

My earliest memories are of the mid-1930s. Hitler had already been in power for two years by the time my own brain started recording the events that became stored in my sub-conscious.

There was, as I remember, great concern among the adults in my family and in the town. The political situation in Germany, the growing persecution, humiliation and degradation of the Jews there was fully reported in the newspapers. So were the riots in Palestine, with the daily killings of Jews by the Arabs. I was an avid reader from the time I learned to read at the age of five. And apart from reading the newspapers at home, I remember being riveted in front of the kiosks eagerly devouring all the printed words. I soon became familiar with the many newspapers and publications on display and subsequently I derived satisfaction from listening to the political discussions that were incessantly taking place. I thus acquired a very early political awareness and a maturity far beyond my years. My mother was an ardent Zionist, and it was at her instigation that in 1935 my parents obtained permits to emigrate to Palestine. My father was about to sell his share in the flour mill. Everyone was primed to leave – until my father found himself in a dilemma – a situation that was mirrored in thousands of other Polish-Jewish families.

My grandmother dissuaded my father from taking what she considered to be a dreadfully final step – it seemed inconceivable to her that he should want to leave Poland with his wife and children for a distant land where riots and disturbances were commonplace and where the future was very uncertain.

My grandmother was more persuasive than my mother. The arrangements were unmade and the tickets were never bought.

From the time my grandmother influenced my father not to start a new life in Palestine, the relationship between her and my mother was severely strained, to the extent that my mother blamed her mother-in-law for all that was to happen to us subsequently. It would be years before I discovered the reason for the coldness between my mother and grandmother, which even now I find embarrassing. During the war, when we sat around at home during the long curfews I pieced together the truth of what happened.

I had always been aware of antisemitism – if only because Jewish boys were constantly being attacked by the Polish boys. There was a gulf between us; even though I may not have looked particularly Jewish – a fact that would help me when I later ran messages to and from the Ghetto in our town.

At this time, however, Poland, the country with the biggest Jewish population in Europe, was in the midst of one of its periodic spells of antisemitism. After the death of Marshal Pilsudski, the right-wing government under Marshal Smigly-Rydz was greatly influenced by the new wave of militant racial nationalism and anti-Jewish agitation increased. Poles were encouraged to boycott Jewish shops, physical attacks on Jews became more frequent and the *numerus clausus*, especially in the Law and Medicine Faculties, was more strictly adhered to.

We lived in a predominantly Jewish environment. We were not particularly religious, although I transferred from the progressive Froebel Kindergarten to the Cheder at the age of 4½ and at six I commenced at the secular school. My paternal grandfather had been extremely Orthodox and pious and spent most of his days learning *Gemara* (the latter part of the Talmud) in the local *shtiebl* (synagogue). My father himself, though, had rebelled at the age of 15, smoked on Saturday and when he did business with the Poles I suspect he ate what the Poles ate (although strict observance of *kashrut*, the Jewish dietary laws, was practised at home).

The Jews of Piotrków reflected the wide spectrum of Jewish political, cultural and religious life. The Zionist organisations were represented by Poale Zion, Hashomer Haz'air, Hashomer Hadati, Hanoar Hazioni, Betar, General Zionists and others.

There was a very active Mizrachi movement.

We also had every strand of Chassidic life, each with its own *shtiebl*. There were the followers of the Gerer Rebbe, the Alexander Rebbe, the Radomsker Rebbe as well as many other renowned Rabbis.

There were non-Chassidic communities, too. The Bundists, who had their own very strong cultural existence, were represented on the Piotrków Town Council by seven councillors. Piotrków was a predominantly Socialist town.

The fabric of Jewish life also included many music circles, literary societies, Yiddish publishing houses, a Jewish gymnasium (grammar school), ORT (vocational training) and a Jewish hospital.

All this from a town that had a population of no more than 50,000. The 15,000 Jews experienced a richness of Jewish life such as people outside Israel in the West today could not begin to fathom – Jewish populations quite as large as that (although not in terms of percentages of the general population) in Britain or France might boast two synagogues and one Zionist society at the most.

In spite of the fact that the Jews lived mainly in their own milieu, there was a growing tendency toward Polonisation. More and more Jews were assuming Polish names and Polish was more frequently spoken especially among the young.

And there was another strand of life in which there was total separation – that of the Jewish beggars, the *shnorrers* as they have come to be known disparagingly in Jewish literature, and the Polish ones. Each had their own separate patch and never the twain did meet. What they had in common was desperate poverty. The scourge of unemployment that hit the world in the 1930s affected Poland to a greater degree, as it was a very poor country, and many Jews who previously supported large families became impoverished and resorted to mendicity.

I will always remember little boys, shoeless, dressed in tatters, going round begging with the hope of nothing more than a crust of bread. I recall on one occasion a boy about my age knocking at our door. I turned him away. My mother called me, and severely reprimanded me, saying, 'You should be grateful that you are not in that position yourself' – and she ensured that I gave the boy more than his crust of bread.

I realised my mistake immediately and have not forgotten its lesson. The incident with the beggar had a profound influence on many of my actions since then.

From a warm home like ours, a flat in an apartment block which to the beggars of the town must have seemed like paradise, the life of the poor was so distant, yet it was part of our everyday existence.

My mother was a woman of sound good common sense, who would quote an epigram pointing to the moral of each experience. She was strict but caring, devoted to her children for whom in the end she gave her life.

My father's business brought him into close contact with the

Polish population with whom he enjoyed a comfortable relationship. They liked him because he was straightforward and they felt at ease with him. He was popular with his employees because he was generous and unassuming – all this stood him in good stead during the terrible days when we were confined to the Ghetto.

The stable life we enjoyed at home came to an end – all too quickly. The date is engraved on my memory – 1 September 1939. That was the day the Germans invaded Poland – the start of the Second World War.

With the ludicrous accusations of Polish aggression against Germany, Nazi troops crossed the frontier and their aircraft bombed Polish targets. We were among the first.

That day, a beautifully warm sunny day, we were staying with my mother's father in Sieradz. It was Friday morning and we had to be back in Piotrków because school was due to begin after the summer holidays on Monday 4 September.

Mother wanted to get home early – so that she could prepare for *Shabbat*, the Sabbath. Fish had to be cooked, the chicken prepared, the table linen and silver just so. The Sabbath is spoken of in Jewish tradition as a bride and it was our duty to welcome her in style.

That *Shabbat* would prove to be horribly different.

Normally the journey between the two places took about two hours by bus. We would leave at seven o'clock in the morning and my father would be waiting to meet us at nine.

No sooner had we got on the bus to begin our journey than there was the sound of aircraft overhead. We knew they were not Polish. Within minutes of hearing the aircraft, there was the more menacing sound of bombs falling. We all left the bus and took what shelter there was in the ditches at the side of the road.

Fortunately, none of us was hurt. But it took eleven hours for the journey to be completed, with my father at one end of the route and my grandfather at the other frantically awaiting news of us.

The following morning, all of us were gathered in the basement of a nearby shop, fearing that the town might be bombed. We didn't have to wait long before the explosions occurred.

Although I was barely ten years old and my two sisters were younger, we were still old enough to react with horror as a man injured by shrapnel was brought into our ready-made shelter. His wounds were extensive and he was smothered in blood.

It was our first experience of the realities of war!!!

After the bombing there was panic. The population of the whole town seemed to be moving east away from the invading army. We were no different. My father hired a carriage, a droshki, and we drove out of town travelling in a pitifully slow procession of humanity.

We turned up at Sulejów, a village of 5,000 people about 15 kilometres away. When we arrived there, it couldn't have looked more peaceful. Certainly, you wouldn't imagine that a hideous war had just begun.

The weather that Sunday was beautiful. Britain declared war that day, but we were totally unable to comprehend that, in our village, life was going to change at all. People were walking around in the warm sunlight as though life really was as serene as the sun made it seem.

I started playing with the local boys. Within minutes I had new friends. A lovely, lovely day – until as the sun began to go down we heard the sound of planes overhead.

They swooped down and started dropping incendiary bombs. Seconds later, this pretty little village was a mass of flame. At ten years of age, I had never seen anything like it before. I have also seen nothing like it since – not even Dante's Inferno could have been visualised in this form. No one knew where to go, but they were all running in different directions, some with their clothes on fire. Blindly running. Cats, dogs, horses, cows, all of them aflame, too, all running. Madly, pointlessly, agonisingly.

Instantly, whole families were consumed by flames. That we managed to escape unhurt was a real miracle.

As we ran into the nearby woods, I could see people falling all around us – picked off by machine guns from the aircraft overhead.

There was the terrible sound of screaming. Sometimes just screams. Sometimes names – 'Moishe!', 'Gittel!' Names that might never be heard again but which at that moment were being called in other towns and villages all over Poland.

Then there were those looking for their children, for parents, for grandparents, for brothers, for sisters. About 3,000 people were burnt and killed within a very short time, whole families wiped out and many decimated. By a miracle our family of five was saved.

Our horse was killed, our carriage destroyed. So my father led us on foot away from the village. We managed to hire a lift in a horse and cart. We moved from village to village until one morning the Germans caught up with us. My parents decided it was time to go back to Piotrków.

There, our home still stood. Our belongings were still intact.

The former synagogue in Piotrków. It is now a library.

Ben Helfgott had been free for only two months when this photograph of him (left) was taken in July 1945.

That November, we were herded into a Ghetto – the first to be established in Poland, a year before the mammoth Warsaw Ghetto was set up.

Our only advantage was that unlike Warsaw or the Ghetto at Lódz, we were not surrounded by a wall. It was an open Ghetto, although there were distinct borders with notices bearing the Nazi death's head, warning Jews not to stray out of the area, into which Poles were forbidden to enter.

For a large sum of money my father obtained a permit which enabled him to move in and out of the Ghetto freely. Although the permit authorised him to purchase rabbit skins (which were used for coats worn by the German Wehrmacht fighting on the Russian Front), he was in fact never engaged in this activity, but it gave him the necessary cover to set up links with the outside world and establish a network to smuggle food into the Ghetto. Helped by the fact that I didn't look Jewish, I used to roam around outside the Ghetto. Although I was well aware of the risks, and fear was always lurking at the back of my mind, I was driven almost obsessively to overcome this challenge, which I foolishly but deliberately accepted. I even used to go to the cinema. I could have been shot for doing that, but the lure of the screen in that darkened building was too strong for a ten/eleven-year-old to resist.

The surrounding population exhibited indifference to our fate rather than enthusiasm. Some derived a kind of *Schadenfreude* from it; the Germans were at last doing what they themselves would have

Ben Helfgott the Olympic athlete
– representing Britain in
weightlifting in the 1956 Games.
Associated Press

possibly wished to do. Others felt sorry for the poor Jews. They
sympathised but could do nothing. Yet others were absolutely
delighted. The Germans were removing this 'foreign' element –
even though many Jews had been there far longer than the 'natives'.

In retrospect, it was a dark chapter in the history of Polish-
Jewish relations. Ignoring the turbulent vicissitudes of the thousand
years of the Jewish sojourn in Poland, the Nazis were, after all, our
common enemy. They had stated quite clearly and unambiguously
that the Slav people were destined for exploitation and subjugation.
Common sense, setting aside personal feelings, decency and
humanity, would have dictated that co-operation was preferable and
of mutual benefit. Admittedly the Nazis were ruthless with those
who were found to give refuge to Jews, but there were many ways in
which succour could have been extended without undue risk and
jeopardy to one's life. Indeed, just minding one's own business would
have saved thousands of lives. Those who did help were honoured
after the war at Yad Vashem in Jerusalem in the Avenue of the
Righteous Gentiles. However, ignorance and prejudice, which had
been nurtured over many centuries, exerted a much greater force
and thus the fate of the Jews was more catastrophic than it might
otherwise have been.

Memories of Romania:
Hermy Jankel

Hermy Jankel was born in Romania and came to Britain as a young married woman after having lived in Israel for the five years up to 1946. She is married to an engineer and is a grandmother. They are active members of the Reform Synagogue movement and Hermy is co-chairman of her local women's Zionist group. They live in London.

Hermy Jankel and her husband Freddy in London, 1987.

Hermy Jankel: I left Romania in 1941. I was 14 years old and my family and I were among the last batch of legal emigrants from the country to enter what was then Palestine.

We left after a series of antisemitic incidents and having had part of our lovely home in Bucharest used as a billet for senior officers of the Wehrmacht, yet I think of the land of my birth still with affection.

I have often wanted to go back there, but it just hasn't worked out. Nevertheless, I have very happy memories of my childhood in

Hermy Jankel's parents on their wedding day in Jassy.

Hermy Kempner aged 10 in 1936.

Romania. Perhaps that is inevitable, because we were a happy family, even though the circumstances of our leaving were anything but pleasant – at a time when Romania's German allies were present in what was in effect 'friendly occupation'.

Actually, I divide my childhood into two parts – up to the age of 11 when most of life seemed perfect and then from 11 to 14 when everything changed, when there was such antisemitism all around that a close schoolfriend was driven to suicide by the taunts and pressures to which she was subjected.

That was in 1938. She went to a state school, which in Romania was the best kind of school, organised on the French system. It was then that things began to change for me. I had got used to the shouts of 'Dirty Jew', but this was when I started to realise that things were going to get much, much worse.

Having Germans around was not all that strange for my parents. My father had studied in Austria and my mother was from a German-speaking family and had studied German at university.

Neither of them looked particularly Jewish, which was useful at a time when the country was ruled by a series of right-wing governments. It was even more useful – but frightening – during the winter of 1940-41 when for two days the whole country was racked by a series of dreadful pogroms.

We were incredibly lucky – because of those billeted German officers who didn't know we were Jewish, were terribly correct and allowed us, like them, to be sheltered by the sentries standing to attention whenever we entered our home. Heels clicked for us as for them. It was not the usual situation for a Romanian-Jewish family in 1940.

A great many of our relatives were not so lucky. In Jassy, where so many of the population were Jewish, an uncle and three cousins of my mother disappeared, never to be seen again.

We were a prosperous middle-class family. My father was a successful import-export merchant and we loved music. Chamber music recitals were frequently held at home, and my father was a great patron of the arts. He had a number of artists under his wing and would give them honoraria to enable them to work. Mother used to do the same with musicians. (To this day, at the age of 89, she still plays the piano beautifully and makes tapes of her performances.)

In the summer of 1938, my parents decided to send me to a French lycée – after having arranged for me to have a French tutor for the three months summer holiday break. By the time the holiday was over, I was fluent in the language and able to take part in the school activities.

Father, who was a great Anglophile (we had a lot of relatives in England; one of my grandfather's brothers lived in Manchester), was the agent for a number of big British concerns in Romania. He also imported many things from Germany. We actually came to England on a visit in 1939 and my parents suggested that I went to school here, but with the approach of war, it couldn't be arranged.

The family lived in what I believed to be a very Jewish environment, although my father was an unbeliever. My mother, though, came from an extremely Orthodox family and because of her, we kept all the high holydays. The only time I remember seeing father in a synagogue was at my son's *barmitzvah*. (He was by then 70 and living in Britain.)

My father went to Palestine on a visit in the 1930s, but was hypercritical of some of the things he saw. My synagogue-going was at first with my mother. We used to go to the Choral Temple in Bucharest, which is now the seat of the Chief Rabbi but was at the

A service at the Choral Synagogue, Bucharest. Hermy preferred the less formal services at the local *shtiebl*.
Jewish Museum, Bucharest

At the Lycée, Bucharest.

time a kind of Conservative synagogue and very fashionable. But I preferred to go with a friend of mine to what I suppose was a sort of *shtiebl*, a prayer room, that always seemed to be filled with devotion. As children, we were very proud of having a new dress and being able to go to enjoy the warm atmosphere of the place. Whereas the Choral Temple was quite a way from us, the *shtiebl* was very close. Simchat Torah, with the sweets and the apples, was lovely there.

I started learning Hebrew at the age of six. I didn't go to *cheder*. What I learned was modern Hebrew, which was very convenient when we came to leave for Palestine.

My mother was a keen Wizo (the Women's Zionist movement) member and went to Palestine in 1935 as a delegate of Romanian Wizo. (I was practically suckled in Wizo and have been co-chairman of my local branch for 30 years.) The Chairman of my mother's group, a Mrs Margolis, was a very prominent figure in local affairs.

My grandmother, who was a very educated and outspoken lady, used to gather unto her unmarried Jewish ladies, one of whom was Anna Pauker, who became the post-war Communist Foreign

Minister of Romania. I knew even then that Jewish people were involved in all sorts of unconventional activities.

My father's younger brother, who was a bachelor until his fifties, was a drawing-room Communist. I remember that when we were young children, we were absolutely certain that when the Russians entered Romania he would at least be Mayor of Bucharest. But it didn't happen and he later went to Israel.

I had a number of non-Jewish friends. There were many diplomats' children at the lycée I attended. My father also, of course, had numerous gentile business associates, but we considered that we were living a totally Jewish life.

We were not, though, a Yiddish-speaking family. There was always a clear division between those who spoke Yiddish and those who did not. I am afraid there was a certain snobbery about that.

Politics was the essence of all conversation and, even as a ten-year-old, I was always aware of what was going on around us. That was how I first became aware that things were going to change for us.

Children were not nursery bound. We were brought up with adults who discussed politics at breakfast, lunch and dinner. We had a German-Jewish governess – someone who my parents discovered needed a job.

The papers were full of antisemitic stories. There were posters damning the Jews on the walls. I was old enough to appreciate the sinister implications of it all.

You couldn't avoid the student rallies and public meetings – the only ones that were allowed – which seemed to concentrate on anti-Jewish ravings. One Sunday, I went to a park and saw one of the meetings under way. It was not a comfortable experience. Free speech wasn't part and parcel of Romanian life. The sort of speeches that were allowed were not encouraging to the Jews.

Things were much worse for those living in Moldavia where the Jewish populations were much larger, in the cluster of small towns and villages there, than were those in Bucharest.

In 1939, once the war started between Britain and Germany, I knew we were going to have to leave, although when it actually happened nearly two years later, somehow I couldn't believe it.

I remember 3 September, when war did break out. I remember it very clearly indeed. It was a beautifully warm sunny day. I was 12 years old, and we were spending the day with friends.

We were very aware that we were being sucked into a political confrontation. And that there was antisemitism all around us.

Romania was a country where everything worked more or less by bribes. People were very corruptible. My father actually bought some baptism certificates which proved that we were all of the true Catholic faith. Father believed in being careful and covering every eventuality.

The two-day pogrom was not an event I will ever forget – although we experienced it from the comfort of our home, behind drawn blinds. But you only had to peep out of those blinds to see the sky red from the burning Jewish property around us. We heard what was going on from our large console radio set, by which we sat practically transfixed all day long, and then there was the shouting in the street outside as the rampaging mobs went in search of their prey. I remember being very frightened. The tree-lined road, Mirceavoda, was a beautiful street and was very close to a Jewish district. We were, of course, protected by our German sentries outside. Our 'tenants' still did not suspect anything about us, or if

A family party at the house in Bucharest.

they did, saw no reason to mind anyone's business but their own.

My father was blond with blue eyes and my mother was fair-haired, too. They belonged to Jewish organisations, but the Germans had not yet started their sophisticated search for Jews, delving into records and such like.

The officers continued to click their heels and act in a correct manner. When we told them that we had sold our house and were leaving, they asked no questions.

We left Romania when a friend of father's at the British Embassy in Bucharest warned that he was on a Romanian government 'list' and would be likely to find things getting difficult for him.

Quite incredibly, he was able to sell his business for a fairly reasonable sum and our entire family, mother, father, my younger sister and I were able to leave, taking with us all our furniture – including a Steinway baby grand – and jewellery.

About twenty members of our family left at this time. We were lucky to have obtained a British Mandate 'certificate'. Only a small number were issued every year as the Arab leadership in Palestine did not want an influx of Jewish immigrants. The certificates were given to families who could prove they had 'means' – which meant that they had access to £1,000.

We went overland to Palestine in the middle of the war – and made the journey amazingly comfortably, stopping to see the sights of Turkey, Syria and Lebanon on the way. How we were able to do so I cannot begin to imagine.

For me it was marvellously exciting. My parents' feelings were probably a lot more mixed.

Jewish Life
in Eastern Europe
Today

Czechoslovakia

Although as many as 15,000 Jews today remain in Czechoslovakia, only about 6,000, the majority over 65, are registered as members of the country's 16 Jewish communities. This discrepancy has a variety of reasons, most of which stem from the anti-religious and anti-Zionist nature of state policy in post-war Czechoslovakia. As long as Communist rule was maintained, especially amongst the younger generation, there was at the very least an anxiety that membership would entail some sort of disadvantage, if not harassment, in the pursuit of their educational or professional careers. Even today, some persons remain unaffiliated out of conviction. An even larger number, probably, are married to non-Jews, which brings to bear another set of reasons why their ties to Jewry might become tenuous.

Until the demise of Communist rule, Jewish communal life remained circumscribed. Even now, aside from maintaining a semblance of religious life and looking after the country's Jewish cemeteries, most organized activity centres around tending to the needs of the increasingly aging membership. In Prague, for instance, a kosher restaurant is maintained at the rococo Prague Jewish Town Hall, and senior citizens with chronic medical problems are sent on visits to health spas, including on occasion to the West, thanks largely to the support of the American Jewish Joint Distribution Committee (the 'Joint') and Central British Fund for World Jewish Relief (the CBF).

The Communist Government, while not actually discouraging the practice of the Jewish religion, kept the Jewish communities of Bohemia, Moravia and Slovakia on a tight tether. Although the authorities had not sanctioned a youth programme as such since the anti-Zionist campaign of the early 1970s, families with children and teenagers did attend Chanukah, Purim and Passover celebrations at the Prague community.

Religious observance, especially in Prague, was given a boost by the installation in 1984 of a young, Budapest-trained Rabbi, Daniel Meyer. Still, he is the only Rabbi in the entire country, including Slovakia where over half of Czechoslovak Jewry actually resides. Except in Prague, where the old synagogues of the former Ghetto are a leading tourist attraction, synagogues, together with other religious and public buildings, are in a sorrowful state of neglect. Over the last years an increasing number of Jewish cemeteries, including one of the older ones in Prague, have been levelled and used as sites for new buildings and parks.

This does not mean, however, that the visitor from the West will find nothing to see of Jewish interest in Czechoslovakia. In Prague, itself, there is what remains of the former Ghetto, located adjacent to the Old Town, where the famous Old Cemetery, Altneu Shul and Jewish Town Hall in addition to several other historically important synagogues (now part of the State Jewish Museum) are to be found. Many synagogues, some quite noteworthy, are even still standing in the small towns and villages, although almost all have been converted for other uses because there are no Jews to worship in them. The same holds true for cemeteries, especially for those which have been deemed to be of historical important by the authorities or are simply on a spot that has escaped development.

The activities of the Jewish communities outside Prague which still function in the Czechoslovak Socialist Republic, also centre mainly on the care of cemeteries and tending to the needs of the ill, indigent and most elderly under the modest welfare programme funded by the 'Joint'. The largest community outside Prague, as one might expect, is in the Slovak capital, Bratislava. Unfortunately, most of what had remained of Jewish interest after the war has been demolished as part of one urban renewal programme or another. One exception, if you can call it that is the grave of the great early nineteenth-century Jewish leader and proponent of traditional Orthodoxy, Rabbi Moses (Hatam) Sofer. Visited mostly by Orthodox and Chassidic Jews who make the trip, especially from nearby Vienna, it is situated beneath an elevated highway, and constitutes together with just a few other graves (some would say miraculously) all that is left of the town's old Jewish cemetery. Access can only be gained by first contacting a caretaker who then guides you down a special set of steps constructed in 1942, during the Hungarian occupation.

A must for any Jewish visitor to Prague still remains Sabbath services at the thirteenth-century Altneu Shul, the oldest European synagogue in use today. Every square inch of its interior reveals the long and rich history of the Jews in the Bohemian Crownlands. Being present at a Torah service within its walls, moreover, is a compelling reminder of the ties that continue to bond not just the remaining Jews of Czechoslovakia, but the whole of Eastern Europe with the rest of world Jewry, from the staunchly anti-Zionist policies it had adopted in the period following the Soviet-led invasion of 1968. Although many people's worst fears were, fortunately, never realized, antisemitism again became a political weapon under the regime of Gustav Husak. Anti-Jewish articles became relatively common in the party press, and as late as the summer of 1987 a rabidly anti-Zionist novel, *The Promised Land*, was published with passages of so offensively antisemitic a nature that the author was taken to court by a Prague lawyer who is a board member of the Union of Anti-Fascist Fighters.

Even though relations with Israel had not really begun to thaw, there were several small, but hopeful signs of change in the last few years of the Communist regime. In 1987, a group of 29 former inmates of Terezin Concentration Camp from Israel were allowed on a commemorative visit, and in 1988 flights of El Al Israel Airlines were once again allowed to fly through Czechoslovak airspace.

There had not been much sign of change at home either, where the authorities maintained their tight grip on Jewish affairs. A clear sign that the Government would not tolerate even the most limited sign of independence came in early 1986 when the term of Dr Desider Galsky as Chairman of the Council of Jewish Communities in Bohemia and Moravia was not renewed and an older man was installed in his place. Galsky was, in fact, not only uniquely capable, but had demonstrated remarkable courage and perseverance in his dealings with the authorities. His frequent trips to the West, partly in association with the tour in the USA of the *Precious Legacy* exhibition of treasures from the Jewish Museum of Prague, made him respected and well-known to Jewish leaders abroad.

An abrupt end to this pattern of repression came with the demise of Communist rule in the so-called 'Velvet Revolution' of November/December 1989. Under the leadership of President Vaclav Havel, himself a former dissident, Czechoslovakia has become the most viable of the emerging democracies of Eastern Europe. No sooner had the Communist regime of Milos Jakes resigned than did the Council of Jewish Communities act to clean its own house. A meeting was held at the old Jewish Town Hall in Prague at which the puppet leadership was deposed and Desider Galsky was reinstated as chairman. A general change in the Council's leadership followed, resulting in the initiation of a full range of Jewish communal activities, most of which would have been prohibited as anti-Communist and pro-Zionist under the previous regime.

Of perhaps even greater practical significance has been the return of the American Jewish Joint Distribution Committee (the JDC or 'Joint') to Czechoslovakia. Only nominally present in recent years, it will now be able to offer a full range of welfare services to the country's increasingly elderly Jewish population.

On the international front, the new Czechoslovak Government has taken the significant step of restoring diplomatic relations with Israel. Additionally, the two most important diplomatic posts of the new regime have been given to persons of Jewish origin. The son of Rudolf Slansky, put to death in the notoriously antisemitic show trials of the 1950s, is the new Czechoslovak ambassador to the Soviet Union and Rita Klimova, a leading dissident and former economics professor, is the new Government's envoy to Washington.

As one would have expected, in contrast to some of the other formerly Communist societies of Eastern Europe, antisemitism has fortunately been almost entirely absent during Czechoslovakia's transition to democracy. This is mostly a reflection of the relative unimportance of Jew-hatred as a force in the political life of pre-war Czechoslovakia. It is also a reaction against repeated attempts by successive Communist regimes to use antisemitism as a vehicle for discrediting their opponents and bolstering their generally unpopular anti-Israel Middle East policy. As a consequence, the Jews remaining in Czechoslovakia, unlike their co-religionists in Hungary or Romania, have had no reason but to welcome the end of Communist rule in their country. Like their non-Jewish friends and neighbours they are confident that for Czechoslovakia the future will bring democratic renewal and economic improvement.

Bratislava (Germ: Pressburg;
Hung: Pozsóny) – once a
thriving centre of Jewish life and
home of a number of great rabbis.
The synagogue is both a
memorial to its past and a
stubborn demonstration that for
some Czechoslovakian Jews there
is a present – if not a future.
Judy Goldhill

There may not be a large congregation and it has no rabbi but for this man at this moment, wrapped in his *tallit* (prayer shawl) Bratislava could be Jerusalem.
Judy Goldhill

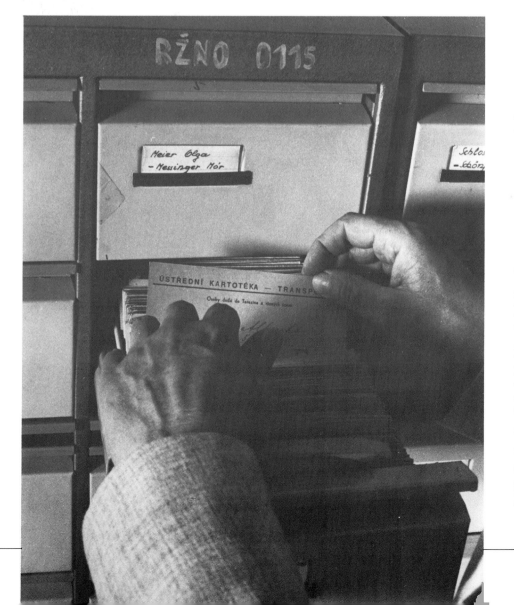

The haunting memory. The monstrous efficiency of the Nazi horror machine comes home all too vividly in the Jewish community centre in Prague. Here are the files, meticulously kept, recording the transportation of Jews to the camp at Theresienstadt (Terezin). Survivors of that infamous place make for the Jewish town hall and find their own cards in this grisly exhibit.
Judy Goldhill

Fritz Gruenwald, the President of
the remnant of the Slovak Jewish
community centring on
Bratislava, in 1987.
Judy Goldhill

**The cemetery at Kosice (Germ:
Kashau; Hung: Kassa).**
Yale Strom/Brian Blue

Right:
The 13th-century Altneu Schul in Prague (literally, the Old New Synagogue) is the oldest synagogue in Europe. Behind it is the Rococo Jewish Town Hall, famous for its two clocks – the lower one has Hebrew characters and the hands turn anti-clockwise.
The Hulton Picture Company

Below:
The Altneu Schul still holds traditional Orthodox services every Sabbath. As seen from the women's gallery.
Judy Goldhill

**Morning service (Shachrit) at the
Bratislava synagogue.**
Yale Strom/Brian Blue

Right:
A Jewish couple at Bratislava.
Yale Strom/Brian Blue

Below:
The kosher kitchen at Bratislava.
Judy Goldhill

Hungary

In marked contrast to the situation in Czechoslovakia is the one in Hungary. With at least 80,000 Jews, the overwhelming majority of whom are in the capital, Budapest, it has the largest Jewish population in the Eastern bloc outside the Soviet Union. With its rich array of Jewish religious and secular institutions, Hungary has, moreover, rightfully been termed by the New York-based Memorial Foundation for Jewish Culture 'the best hope for the revival of the Jewish people in Eastern Europe'.

Although the contrast with the rest of the region can be explained solely in demographic terms, the unique status of the Hungarian Jewish community has also to be seen in the wider political context. Under the leadership of Janos Kadar, following the ill-fated revolution of 1956, the Hungarian Communist Party pursued a policy which aimed at the creation of what might be called a 'tacit consensus'. In other words, the Hungarian people were asked to accept their fate as a one-party Communist state within the Soviet orbit in return for a measure of freedom and choice within the economic and cultural spheres. Kadar's system of 'Goulash Communism', as it has been termed because of its emphasis on the provision of ample supplies of food and consumer goods, has in part also been motivated by the desire to improve relations with the West, in particular better economic ties with the United States for whom the treatment of Jews and other minorities has always been an important criterion in its relations with the countries of the Eastern bloc.

It can be argued that, all in all, the Jews of Hungary have benefited considerably, also in economic terms, from the policies pursued by the Kadar regime, and now the government of Grosz. Not only have the authorities tolerated, and lately even encouraged, Jewish studies (partly financed by the Memorial Foundation for Jewish Culture), but the Kadar economic policy of encouraging small businesses, providing incentives for managers and rewarding physicians, scientists, engineers and other professionals with relatively high salaries has helped bolster the traditionally Jewish middle classes of Hungary.

The problem is, however, that, as elsewhere in the Eastern bloc, only fewer than half of the Jews in the country, and mostly the elderly at that, are registered with the Jewish community. While this is, admittedly, in many ways the consequence of 'assimilationist' tendencies that, as discussed earlier, began even before the First

World War, the trend towards non-affiliation was encouraged by factors similar to those operating in Czechoslovakia. In the first place, no matter how unorthodox the post-revolutionary regimes of Hungary may have been in their economic and cultural policies, until recently the basic outlines of Communist one-party rule were maintained and the country remained firmly within the Soviet orbit. This meant, put succinctly, that in no way was it advantageous to be a professing Jew. At the very least, registration with the Jewish community had the potential of discrimination in employment and education.

Moreover, even though Kadar generally kept his country on the sidelines of the Soviet-led anti-Zionist campaign following the Six-Day War and, in September 1989, Hungary became the first Warsaw-pact state to restore diplomatic ties with Israel, antisemitism has remained a noticeable undercurrent in the country. It is strong amongst populist-oriented writers and intellectuals who share some of the nativist views of the pre-war far Right, as well as amongst elements in Hungarian society jealous of Jewish success in the economy and professions. With many Jews having been prominent in the Hungarian Communist leadership, antisemitism has also become linked with anti-Communism. As long as Communist rule remained intact it found no other mode of public expression than jokes and jibes by individuals. Observers described the situation as one in which there was no antisemitism, but only antisemites. As Hungary has been evolving into a multi-party democracy antisemitism has once again regrettably become an element in political discourse. This was particularly evident in the campaign leading up to the country's first free elections since 1945, held in March and April 1990. Despite all assertions of the party leadership to the contrary, it was an unmistakable sub-text of the campaign conducted by the populist wing of Hungarian Democratic Forum, the election's right-of-centre victors. Examples that come most readily to mind are the outbursts of the popular playwright Istvan Csurka against an unnamed 'clique' of 'Leninists' as well as his use of the slogan 'Hungarians Awake', and the references in Hungarian Democratic Forum's party journal to the rival political grouping, the Free Democrats, as 'inbred democrats, detached from the people and the people's soil' and 'rootless cosmopolitans'. Also, stars of David and swastikas were scrawled on some of the Free Democrats' posters. One should perhaps note that antisemitism has been just one more reason why many Jews, if they do so at all, express their Jewishness only in private.

And yet, in Hungary none of the accoutrements of a traditional Jewish life is missing. Budapest alone boasts thirty synagogues and houses of prayer, Talmud Torahs, a number of rabbis, a *mohel* (ritual circumcisor), a Jewish day school, a ritual slaughter house, kosher butchers, a *matzoh* bakery, a *mikveh* (ritual bath), a kosher restaurant, and, perhaps most significant of all, the only Jewish theological seminary in the Eastern bloc. Religious life in the capital is centred in the magnificent 130-year-old Dohany Street Synagogue where about 200 worshippers gather each sabbath. There are, additionally, sizeable communities of practising Jews in Szeged, Miskolc, Debrecen, Gyor and Pec. Although most of the Jews in Hungary today follow the Neolog trend in Jewish observance (similar to the United Synagogue of the UK or the Conservative movement of the USA), there is also a significant Orthodox minority centred in Budapest which has its own *Beth Din* (rabbinic court), slaughter house, houses of worship and, most recently, its own Rabbi who comes from Israel and is a follower of the Satmar sect of Chassidim.

All Jewish activity is coordinated by the Central Board of Hungarian Jews, which is also responsible for conveying government policy on religious matters to all Jews. In that sense, its function is broadly similar to that of the umbrella organizations of Czechoslovak Jewry. The difference is that it operates under the guidance of 300 elected members who, in turn, elect a 47-member governing council.

As in Czechoslovakia, the Jewish community's activities are financed in large measure by the state, partly through the collection of religious taxes. Outside help in the form of a yearly subsidy in excess of $1 million is received each year from the 'Joint' and CBF to pay for the necessarily large social welfare programme, to care for the needs of the country's increasingly aging Jewish population. What is most unusual about this subsidy is that since 1980 it has been received under a directly negotiated contract between the 'Joint', the Hungarian Department for Church Affairs and the Central Board of Hungarian Jews. It should be mentioned, too, that the funding is received and administered by the independently-constituted Central Committee for Social Assistance.

The institution which, at least till quite recently, has perhaps best reflected the pluralist nature of Hungary's Jewish policy has been Budapest's Jewish Theological Seminary. Under the magnetic leadership until his passing in 1985 of Rabbi Alexander Scheiber, it became not only a centre of learning and scholarship, but a gathering place for those amongst Budapest's younger generation of Jews who were concerned with finding some way of intellectually and socially preserving their Jewishness. Rabbi Scheiber would host an *Oneg* each Friday evening after *Kabbalat Shabbat* for some 200 people. After making *kiddush* (blessing the sabbath wine), reciting the *mozi* (the blessing for bread) and passing around chunks of *challah* (sabbath bread, usually plaited), he would customarily give a talk on that week's Torah portion or on some topic of Jewish interest – a new book perhaps, or an item in the news. Although afterwards a number of Hebrew songs would be sung, these gatherings in order to continue had to be devoid of Zionist content. They have continued under Scheiber's successor, Rabbi Josef Schweitzer.

Despite the success of Scheiber and now Schweitzer in providing a focus for Jewish youth in Budapest, the fact remains that the community as a whole is over-aged. While official sources have not been forthcoming with demographic data, knowledgeable sources estimate that there are about 2000 deaths per year and only 100 births. It remains to be seen whether the continued softening of government policy will help create an environment in which the long-term decline in the Jewish population will be abated, if not reversed.

Leisure time at a youth shelter set up in Hungary in 1946.
Peretz Revesz, Israel

Learning in the Hebrew school
(*cheder*) run by the Orthodox
congregation at the Kacinczy
synagogue is not all dusty books.
Yale Strom/Brian Blue

Marta Landsman has owned a hat
shop in the old Jewish quarter of
Budapest since 1946.
Yale Strom/Brian Blue

The Dohany Synagogue.
Central British Fund

A sight to make a Jewish heart beat faster. The vast Yom Kippur congregation at the Dohany Synagogue, Budapest, the largest Jewish house of prayer in Europe and the second largest synagogue in the world.
Central British Fund

The Ghetto Memorial in Budapest – in the courtyard of the Dohany Synagogue.
Central British Fund

The Hannah Senesh plaque in the Dohany Synagogue, Budapest – with the Shammas (beadle) of the synagogue.
Central British Fund

**Talmudical discussion at the
Orthodox Kacinczy Synagogue in
Budapest.**
Yale Strom/Brian Blue

The Ujpest Synagogue, Hungary.
Central British Fund

The late Satmar Rebbe, Rabbi Joel Teitelbaum (seated centre), on a visit to Budapest in 1970.
Jewish Museum, Budapest

**Jewish choir's recital at the Pava
Centre, Budapest.**
Judy Goldhill

**Morning service inside a
Budapest Orthodox synagogue.**
Yale Strom/Brian Blue

Simchat Torah (the Rejoicing of the Law festival) at the Dohany Synagogue, Budapest 1980.
Jewish Museum, Budapest

Rabbi Alexander Scheiber was called Hungarian Jewry's 'Treasure'. Dr Scheiber was Director of the Institute for Rabbinical Studies, the principal training centre for East European rabbis. The picture was taken shortly before his death in 1985.

There is still a core of ultra-Orthodox Jews living in Hungary. Here, the grandson of Rabbi Sajele Steiner gathers with followers around the rabbi's underground grave at Bodrogveresztur on his *yarzeit*, the anniversary of his death – in April 1985.
José Andrés Lacko

A service at the Temple of Heroes, built by the Jewish community of Budapest in honour of the 10,000 Jews who died fighting for their country in the First World War.
Joint Distribution Committee

Rabbi Alfred Schoner is pleased
to note that these children in the
local Hebrew classes (*cheder*)
know most of the answers.
Judy Goldhill

Sabbath eve in Budapest.
Tamas Féner

Preparing *challot* (the special Sabbath loaves) under rabbinical supervision in Budapest.
Yale Strom/Brian Blue

Rabbi Josef Schweitzer of the
Rabbinical Theological Seminary
in Budapest teaching a father and
son after school.
Yale Strom/Brian Blue

An Orthodox wedding in
Budapest.
Tamas Féner

Poland

Paradoxically, the country in Eastern Europe which today has the smallest Jewish population, before the Holocaust had the largest. Out of a pre-war Jewish population in Poland of 3.5 million, only 12–15,000 Jews, two-thirds of whom are not registered as Jewish, currently remain in the country. The largest single community is not in the capital, Warsaw, but in the formerly-German city of Wrocław (Breslau) in Western Poland, where many Jews from the eastern part of the country ceded to the Soviet Union made their home after the Second World War. Significant numbers of Jews also reside in such former major centres of Jewish population as Lódz, Katowice, Czestochowa, Sosnowiec, Walbrzych and Lublin.

Unlike in the other countries of the Soviet bloc, organized Jewish activity in Poland, in part reflecting the diversity of life in the community prevailing in the country before the war, is run by two separate bodies. Religious activity is in the hands of the Union of Religious Congregations, while secular endeavours are the responsibility of the Jewish Cultural and Social Union. The two organizations, however, have a close working relationship. They have, for example, formed a special commission to coordinate relief activities, the funding of which was resumed by the 'Joint' and CBF in late 1981 after a hiatus of fourteen years. One might add that the head of the Jewish Cultural and Social Union, the Yiddish theatre director Szymon Szurmiej, was elected to Parliament in October 1986 and has been a delegate to the World Jewish Congress.

As in the rest of the region, most Jews are of advanced age. Not just the Holocaust, but successive waves of Jewish emigration since the liberation, the last one following the anti-Jewish campaign of 1968 under President Gomulka, have meant that Jews have virtually disappeared from a society in which they at one time represented 10 per cent of the general population.

Despite this sad demographic fact, successive Polish Governments have improved relations with Israel and instituted a programme to preserve what remains of the Jewish presence in Poland. This process culminated with the re-establishment of diplomatic relations between Poland and Israel on 27 February 1990. There have also been a number of significant visits under the banner of cultural exchange. Both the Bat Dor Ballet company and the Israel Philharmonic have embarked on performance tours of Poland with corresponding visits of Polish companies to Israel. For the first time in over twenty years, as well, Israeli youth groups have begun visiting Poland.

As part of its programme to preserve for posterity the Jewish contribution to Polish society and culture, the authorities have undertaken to restore synagogues. They have encouraged, as well, the mounting of exhibitions and other cultural events designed to correct the largely negative image Jews have enjoyed till now across the broad spectrum of the Polish population. In 1987 alone, a Jewish film festival was held in Kraków, a Judaica exhibit was opened at the State Archaeological Museum in Warsaw and a 'week of Jewish culture' was organized at the Catholic University of Lublin. Excerpts from Claude Lanzmann's monumental film on the Holocaust, *Shoah*, were shown on Polish television. Largely critical of Poles as bystanders in the extermination process, the film was followed by a lively studio discussion. For weeks afterward, Lanzmann's depiction of Polish complicity in the 'Final Solution' was the subject of heated public debate, which tended to criticize the film-maker for his inability to understand that Poles, too, suffered under the Nazi occupation and were just not in a position to help Jews on a massive scale. One might add that this debate has taken place between Poles and Jews outside Poland as well.

Intertwined with this programme of preserving and coming to terms with the past has been a series of international scholarly conferences held in Poland, the United States, Britain and, most recently, in Israel on the history of Polish Jewry. In Poland, the conference took place in 1987 at the Jagellonian University of Kraków, which used the occasion to announce the establishment of an institute for the study of the history and culture of Polish Jews. Perhaps the most visible 'remnant' of the glory that was Jewish culture in Poland is the State Yiddish Theatre in Warsaw. Directed by the legendary Szymon Szurmiej and consisting of a largely non-Jewish acting troupe, it plays a rich repertoire of Yiddish-language works for the stage to packed houses of non-Jews who follow what is going on via earphones with simultaneous Polish translations. Recently, a number of Yiddish classics, including several works of the Nobel laureate Isaac Bashevis Singer, have appeared in Polish translation.

It is a matter for conjecture what exactly brought about this change in Polish policy towards Jews and Israel. Some would argue that it resulted from a sincere desire on the part of the authorities to recognize the role played by Jews in the history and culture of Poland. Others wonder whether the Jaruzelski Government's shift was not, indeed, part of an international public relations exercise intended to win over Jewish opinion-makers and business people in the West, especially because it could thereby be seen to occupy the moral higher ground *vis-à-vis* the embattled Solidarity Movement whose right-wing fringe harboured some antisemitic elements. No matter what the true motives behind this shift may have been, it represented a break from the attitude of earlier Polish governments, including those since the establishment of Communist rule after the war, which rather than trying to come to terms with the scourge of antisemitism in their country exploited it for political purposes.

In this context, it can only be hoped that the recent controversy surrounding the establishment of a Carmelite convent at the site of Auschwitz concentration camp will not have developed beyond being a glitsh in this process of reconciliation. Most disturbing of all, of course, was the August 1989 homily of the Polish Primate, Cardinal Glemp, which in its harsh criticism of efforts by Jewish groups to remove the convent evoked the language and tone of pre-war Polish antisemitism:

> *Do not talk with us from the position of a people raised above all others . . . If there would be no 'anti-Polonism', there would be no antisemitism in this country . . . [there have been] businessmen who neglected and detested Poles . . . Your power lies in the mass media that are easily at your disposal in many countries.*

While the convent crisis thus confirmed the reality of Polish antisemitism, by occasioning positive responses from the Solidarity leadership, from Polish leaders abroad and from Catholics all over the world, it propelled the dialogue between Jews and Poles to a new level of frankness and understanding. In that sense, it most probably heralds the start of a new era in Polish–Jewish relations, including outside Poland itself. The only problem is that it has come at a point when the Jewish community of Poland is all but a slim shadow of its former self.

The Nozyk Synagogue in
Warsaw, which is still in use.
Stanislaw Krajewski

The Rema Synagogue in Kraków,
showing the Ark. Note the *tallit*,
or prayer shawl, draped over a
front pew.
Stanislaw Krajewski

The now-ruined synagogue of
Rymanow in the Rzeszow
province of Galicia. It was built
in the 16th century.
Jacob Weizner

Passover seder at the home of the
Krajewski family in 1984.
Monika Krajewska

Working out his shopping list –
the organizer of the Jewish food
distribution centre in Warsaw.
Judy Goldhill

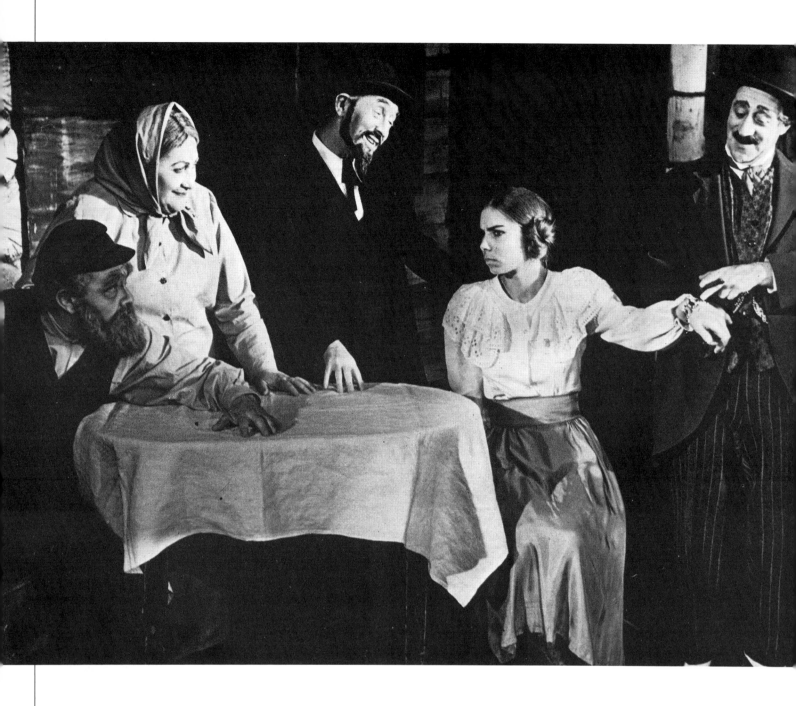

Fiddler on the Roof. The original
Sholem Aleichem story on which
this was based, *Tevye the
Milkman,* performed at the
Warsaw Yiddish Theatre – still
thriving, even though several of
the performers are not Jewish.

Right:
One of the leaders of the Polish Jewish community, 1984.
Judy Goldhill

Below:
Moshe Finkelstein, head of the Polish Jewish community in 1987.
Judy Goldhill

Above:
The Ghetto Memorial in
Warsaw. Dr Akiva Kohane,
Director of the Joint Distribution
Committee in Poland, has just
recited Kaddish (the Jewish
memorial prayer) there.
Judy Goldhill

Left:
The Umschlagplatz memorial.
The German name no Polish
Jewish survivor will ever forget.
It was there they were gathered
for transportation to Auschwitz.
Judy Goldhill

Diners at the Warsaw kosher
canteen.
Judy Goldhill

Above:
One Jewish ritual that continues
– a funeral in Warsaw.
Yale Strom/Brian Blue

David Kagen and his daughter
Irene sing Yiddish folk songs in
Wroclaw (Germ: Breslau).
Yale Strom/Brian Blue

Romania

Until the recent upheaval in Eastern Europe and fall of the Ceauscescu regime, the country with arguably the best record on its treatment of Jews was Romania. Under the ousted and executed President and Communist Party First Secretary, a benevolent policy towards Jews and Israel was an integral part of Ceauscescu's effort to steer his country along a course of independence from Moscow in foreign affairs. Two of the main touchstones of this policy – the maintenance of diplomatic relations with the State of Israel and the fostering of close ties with the United States – had been intertwined with the way in which the Romanian government treated its Jewish population. Emigration to Israel has reached the point that by now 380,000 Romanians have already gone on *aliyah*, with over a thousand still leaving yearly. The Jews remaining in Romania, which estimates put at between 26,000 and 70,000, as compared to about 800,000 before the war, enjoyed the best status of any Jewish population under a Communist government.

The extent to which Ceauscescu had been able to build up political capital amongst world Jewry could be seen in the reaction of American Jewish leaders to the US Congress's threat to suspend Romania's 'Most Favoured Nation' trade status for its maltreatment of ethnic minorities, especially Hungarians. They lobbied Congress not to do so, fearing, of course, that Romanian Jewry would suffer the consequences.

At least in part the fears of the American Jewish leaders were also aroused by the appearance in Romania, supposedly ruled by Ceauscescu's iron fist, of a spate of antisemitic literary works and newspaper articles. Aimed to some extent against the well-known Chief Rabbi Moses Rosen, because of his protest against the publication of the complete works of the virulently antisemitic Romanian national poet Eminescu, the campaign was heralded by an article in a literary weekly by the writer Corneliu Vadim. Attacking Rosen personally, it even referred to his wearing nineteenth-century clothing that smelt, and to Jews in general for being a foreign element that had no business meddling in Romanian culture. For a time, there was speculation that these attacks were part of a scheme to depose Ceauscescu. Still others put forward the theory that the Romanian leader himself or some members of his inner circle deliberately stirred up antisemitic passions in order to divert public attention away from the country's disastrous economic situation. Even though Ceauscescu himself did eventually speak out against Jews, suffice it to say that the hatred of Jews remains encrusted in the fabric of Romanian nationalism and as such will not readily disappear.

Although the sudden upsurge of antisemitism sent shock waves through the country's remaining Jews, it in no way endangered their 'protected' status in Romanian society. Religious life continued in all its diversity, from the orthodox Moldavian communities of Dorohoi, Botosani and Jassy to the Neolog congregations in the formerly Hungarian cities of Cluj (Klausenburg), Orodea and Timisoara (Temesvar). Synagogues were repaired and the Talmud Torahs still educated the young. Perhaps most important of all are the Community's welfare programmes, supported by the 'Joint' and CBF to the tune of $3.5 million yearly, which ensure that the increasingly aging population will grow old in dignity. Their health is cared for in a number of old-age homes, including one opened several years ago with hospital facilities in Bucharest.

Much of the credit for this state of affairs belongs to Chief Rabbi Moses Rosen, who since 1963 has also been President of the Federation of Jewish Communities. An ex-officio Member of Parliament and called by some the 'Red Rabbi' for his good relations with the Romanian Communist leadership, he has been an indefatigable defender of Jewish interests in his country. It was largely his influence that prevented Communist Party members from holding leadership posts in the community. A convinced Zionist, Rabbi Rosen has, nevertheless, always worked hard to maintain the traditional fabric of Jewish life at home. As you will be able to read later in Rosen's own words, it is the continued vitality of Jewish life in Romania that goes a long way to explain why the overwhelming majority of Romanian Jews leaving the country settle permanently in Israel rather than seeking their fortunes elsewhere in the world.

What the future holds in store for the Jews remaining in Romania now that the repressive regime of Ceauscescu has been toppled is at this point still a matter for speculation. As elsewhere much will depend on whether or not the reform movement will bring about some form of democratic and pluralist rule.

In the unlikely event that a new wind blows from Moscow and reaction sets in, it is conceivable that the restoration of repressive regimes of Eastern Europe would occasion a return to the anti-Jewish measures of the past. There is also concern that as each of the societies under review becomes more pluralist in character, faces economic difficulties as a consequence of liberalization and experiences outpourings of nationalism, these upheavals could lead to the emergence of one form or another of antisemitism. Much ultimately also depends on the international situation. To a great extent the treatment of Jews in Eastern Europe since the war has been intertwined with developments in the Middle East. There is every reason to believe, therefore, that the ongoing improvement in relations will continue and we can only hope that the anti-Zionist campaigns of the post-1967 era will not occur again.

No matter how much political and economic conditions may eventually improve, it is hard to envision anything like a rebirth of Jewish life taking place in Hungary, or for that matter elsewhere in the region. The demographic realities of the situation make the possibility of such a revival on anything but a limited scale little more than an illusion.

Dr Moses Rosen has been Chief Rabbi of Romania since 1948, longer than any other Jewish religious leader in the world. He also, by virtue of his office, sits in the Romanian Parliament, the National Assembly. He was officially welcomed to the building on his installation by Emil Bodnaras, Deputy Premier and Minister of Defence – a gesture that indicated that the official Romanian line was not antisemitic.

Jewish Museum, Bucharest

The entrance to the Merarske
Shihl Synagogue in Jassy.
Zusia Efron, Jerusalem

A *cheder* – Hebrew class – at
Jassy.
Zusia Efron, Jerusalem

Above:
The unique situation of Romania as a viable Jewish centre in the midst of the Eastern bloc brought a steady stream of visitors from the West, and from Israel in particular. Here, Golda Meir, then Prime Minister of Israel, hears Chief Rabbi Moses Rosen preaching at the Choral Synagogue in Bucharest during her visit to Romania in May 1972.
Jewish Museum, Bucharest

Right:
Menachem Begin followed Golda Meir's example by coming to worship at the Choral Synagogue when he visited Bucharest in August 1977. He is carrying a scroll of the Torah, accompanied by the Chief Rabbi of Romania, Dr Moses Rosen.
Jewish Museum, Bucharest

Left:
Market day in Radauti 1975
Laurence Salzmann

Below:
Blowing the shofar – the ram's
horn – during Rosh Hashanah
New Year services in Radauti.
Laurence Salzmann

Chief Rabbi Moses Rosen in his
study in Bucharest. They call
him 'His Eminence' – a
somewhat un-Jewish term! What
he has done for his community,
however, is eminent in any
context.
Judy Goldhill

**The Rosen Home in Bucharest.
Looking after the elderly is the
number-one priority in all of
Eastern Europe's Jewish
communities.**
Judy Goldhill

The sure sign that Jewish life is going to continue in Romania – a circumcision ceremony *(brit milah)* in the Kern family at Radauti.
Laurence Salzmann

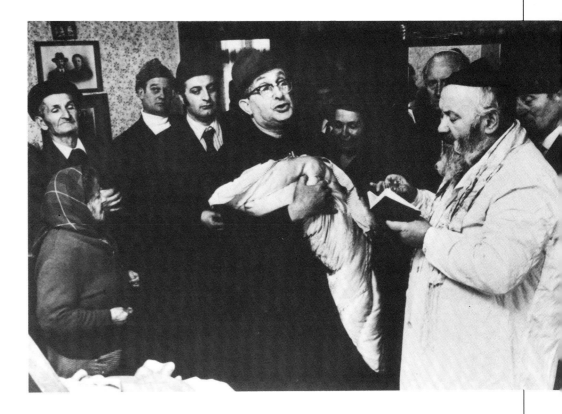

Etta and Abraham Kern at their dining table at Radauti.
Laurence Salzmann

Left:
The Jewish community sees that everyone has the chance of a kosher meal – in the restaurant of the Jewish community in the 'shtetl' of Dorohoi.
Jewish Museum, Bucharest

Below:
Kosher meals on wheels. Ready for the off in Bucharest.
Judy Goldhill

There are no Jewish youth clubs
in Romania, no Zionist groups.
But they have some of the finest
Jewish youth choirs anywhere.
This one in Pietr Neamt,
Moldavia.
Judy Goldhill

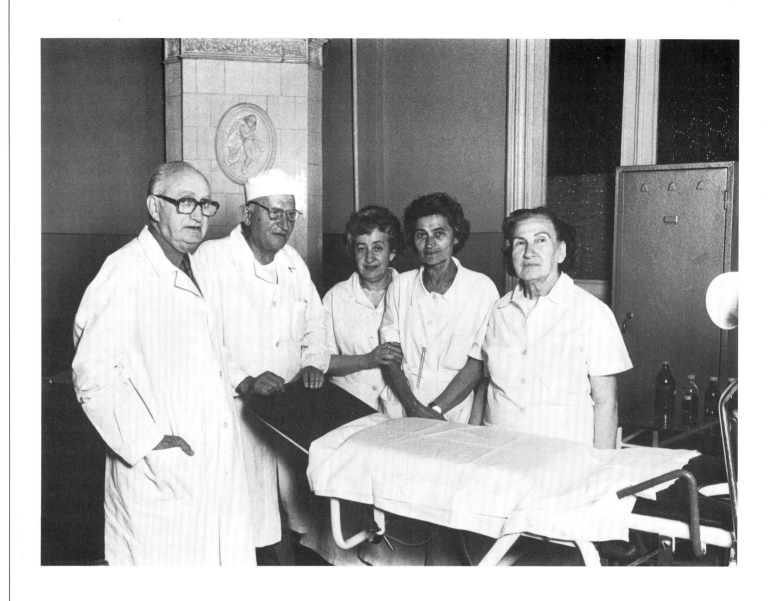

Among the proudest boasts of the
Jewish community is that it runs
one of the finest hospitals in
Romania. Here is part of the
medical team – like its patients,
aged.
Judy Goldhill

**Purim at the Choral Synagogue
in Bucharest.**
Central British Fund

Above:
Purim is the time for Purimspiels – one of the oldest Jewish traditions, a satirical play. This one by the Bucharest Yiddish theatre.
Yale Strom/Brian Blue

Left:
In a world of the past, there is still a future. A Jewish boy in Moldavia. Exactly what it is that he is thinking about is a different matter.
Judy Goldhill

Epilogue

Written in 1987, and at the author's request left unaltered.

The Recipe Rabbi Moses Rosen

Rabbi Moses Rosen

An ancient Jewish folk legend tells us about a mysterious river called **Sambation**. Its violently seething and foaming waters raise high up into the sky a wall of fire and smoke that is impossible to pass through. Beyond, on the other side of the river – the legend goes on – the ten tribes of Israel live, lost in the *terra incognita*. They yearn after us, but we cannot overcome the 'Fire Curtain' in order to reach them. What does the legend call these brothers of ours? 'DIE ROITE YIDDELECH' – 'The little red Jews'.

Si non è vero è bene trovato. How red are the millions of Jews living beyond the Sambation of our times, which – in the language of the late twentieth century – we call the 'Iron Curtain', is something that is known only to themselves and, besides, it is not important. What is important is that, for decades now, the Jewish people of Europe have been divided into two camps, by means of artificial barriers. 'Those on the other side' are expecting the message of those on this side and the latter encounter all sorts of obstacles on the way.

The present volume is the result of the effort made by a group of English Jews who, without wearing the emblem of any local or world organisation and without resorting to any uproar or propaganda, decided to take advantage of the improved conditions for visiting Eastern Europe in order to travel to these communities and try to find out what is happening to the 'little red Jews' of the twentieth century.

They also visited Romania. They roamed about the *shtetlech* – the classic Jewish 'townlets' in Moldavia and Bukovina – they entered our Synagogues where they talked to people, they went to the Talmud Torah classes of our communities and listened to the voices of our children learning the Torah. Our orchestras and our choirs of boys and girls – gay and full of optimism – filled their hearts with joy. The 'explorers' had meals in our ritual restaurants, where almost four thousand persons have lunch daily; they visited our modern and beautiful old people's homes, where nearly 500 persons spend their life's twilight in serene and easy circumstances; they looked for . . . beggars, but could not find a single one, for a subsistence minimum is guaranteed to all by an assistance programme of the Federation of Jewish Communities together with the noble American Jewish Joint Distribution Committee (the 'Joint').

Within the boundaries of Romania, it was impossible for them to discover the isolating 'Sambation' of the 'little red Jews'. Instead, they found a Jewish bi-monthly journal in Romanian, Hebrew, English and Yiddish, published regularly since 1956, in ten thousand copies, mailed *legally* to the Soviet Union, where it is xeroxed in thousands of copies; they found a community visited by the Prime Minister of Israel, by the leaders of the great Jewish world organisations, etc; besides, they realised that almost all Jews living in Romania had already visited Israel and that tens of thousands of Israeli tourists were coming to Romania every year.

Our guests were faced by one enigma after another. Where was the 'fire curtain'? How had it been possible to solve all those specifically religious problems in the framework of a socialist society? And then there was the big question. Where were the 400,000 Romanian Jews who had miraculously survived the Holocaust? At their request, I gave them the latest statistics which show a number of approximately 22,000 Jews now living in Romania, i.e. only 3 per cent of those who lived on this territory 40 years ago. Where were the others? Where had the 97 per cent disappeared to?

Well, our guests again met with surprise after surprise. They went to Israel, where there are now about 400,000 Romanian Jews who constitute a valuable element in the work of rebuilding the 'Holy Land'.

'Good Lord!' exclaimed the 'messengers', who had expected to find there a disaster, assimilation, the disappearance of Judaism, persecution, and numberless similar things described by certain newspapers during the years of the cold war. 'Is it possible that our host should be not only a Rabbi, but also a wizard? All that we see is unreal, totally different from what we have seen elsewhere beyond the Sambation. The Jewish problem – solved. How can that be? What is happening? What are the means resorted to by our host for achieving such a success? What is the recipe he has been using? Is this a dream or reality?

'Can everything we have seen be like Potemkin's villages?

'If not, what is *the recipe?*'

The recipe – that is just what I want to explain and it is my duty to do so. The 22,000 Jews – most of them aged – who have remained and among whom 1400–1500 persons annually continue to leave, no longer carry great weight in world Judaism.

Our importance lies in the fact that the experience of Judaism in Romania provides a practical answer to a vital problem of present-day Jewish life.

That is the problem No. 2 of our times. The problem No. 1 is, of course, the consolidation and development of the State of Israel, which means 'to be or not to be' for the entire Jewish people, irrespective of its whereabouts – East or West, in capitalist or in socialist society.

Problem No. 2 is the following:

Millions of Jews live in Eastern Europe, in a socialist society. No matter if one likes this or not, it represents a reality.

Can Jewish life continue for those millions of brothers and sisters of ours? Should only those who leave be the focus of our attention and are the others – those who remain – doomed to assimilation, to disappearance? Can they, somehow, remain Jewish?

The answer given by the past 40 years of the life led by a Jewish community in socialist Romania is categorical and irrefutable.

Yes, indeed. *They can.* Our 'balance-sheet' proves that, without any noise, demonstrations or rows, we have succeeded in making Romania's interests correspond to ours, and not against the country's leaders, but with their full approval; the result is that, at the same time, 'Aliya', on the one hand, and perfect Judaic religious-cultural freedom and social assistance, on the other hand, have developed and now look exactly as our guests have seen them.

I was young and inexperienced when, in 1948, I was given the responsibility of the destiny of the 400,000 Jews who were the 'remnants' of the Holocaust. I have never been and am not a Kremlinologist, I am no 'specialist' in the matter, and I have not had and have not at present any 'connections' which might have offered me particular possibilities. But I did know one axiomatic truth, namely that success was possible only by making our interests coincide with theirs. *Do ut des*, goes the Latin saying. Give and take.

General de Gaulle used to say: 'I have no enemies, I have no friends, I have interests.'

I succeeded in convincing the Romanian Government that, by doing good to the Jews, by meting out justice to them, it could obtain advantages in matters of favourable public opinion, trade relations, political sympathies.

That is what happened. The 'business transaction' was profitable to both sides.

What can this successful experience teach us?

(1) Out of the two methods – the noisy one based on the slogan 'Let my people go!' and the one we used, that of persuasion – it was ours that succeeded and the first one almost went bankrupt.

(2) Above all, before Aliya, what is important is to maintain the Judaic character of the Jews living in the Soviet Union. Otherwise, if we limit ourselves to 'Let my people go!', we are resorting to a slogan which may be of any kind: touristic (i.e. let us travel), political (i.e. we want to leave a socialist country), but in no case Zionist.

In the first place there is the problem of educating the young people, of maintaining religion, culture, etc, of preventing the last spark of Jewishness, *dus pintale id* – the untranslatable folk definition of the last glimmer of Jewish soul – from going out.

Therefore, 'If you want Olim, you need Jews'. Otherwise it means putting the cart before the horse.

More than 90 per cent of the Romanian Jews reached Lod. They did not 'lose their way' heading for other continents, because they had had Talmud Torah, because their aim had been not emigration, but Aliya; that is to say, they had not fled Romania, their purpose had been the rebuilding of Jerusalem.

(3) The present legislation of the Soviet Union has given us sufficient possibilities of demanding, first and foremost, to have the same rights as the other faiths. If I were to mention only the example of organisation and hierarchy, it would still be quite conclusive. Whereas the Orthodox, the Catholics, the Protestants, the Muslims have organised units (bishoprics, metropolitan seats, patriarchate, etc), the Jewish religion has no legal organisation. That is the beginning of any attempt at reconstructing a Jewish life. If we add that Jewish believers have not a single publication, while the other faiths in the USSR have; if we broach the problem of the thorough training of theological staff – another field in which the Jewish religion is in a state of crass inferiority as compared to the other ones – there is enough legal material for obtaining improvements, for being able to take the first step with a view to a change for the better.

But both at Brussels I and at Brussels II (meetings of the World Conference on Soviet Jewry), we launched only one slogan: Repatriation, Let my people go! Our Resolutions implied that this slogan proclaimed we were forsaking the millions who remained there: 'If they don't leave, we are no longer interested in them.'

The total lack of realism of this policy can be understood by means of a simple calculation, accessible to anybody.

Supposing that our appeals were accepted one hundred per cent and that forty or even fifty thousand Jews left the USSR every year (which would mean an impossible task for Israel, under the present conditions), supposing that all these people reached Israel (which is another Utopia), not taking into account the annual demographic growth of the Jewish population (at least 30,000 – which means that the decrease due to emigration is compensated by the number of births), it would mean that 50 to 60 years would be necessary for the Aliya of approximately three million Jews. In the meantime, will there be a trace of a single Jew left there? Already now their assimilation is almost complete. A few more years and the problem will no longer exist.

Perestroika? Glasnost? I was recently in the Soviet Union, being invited by the Patriarch of the Russian Orthodox Church to attend the celebrations occasioned by the millennium of that Church. When one is there, when one sees with one's own eyes and hears with one's own ears the proportions of the revolution that has taken place there, the radical transformations in mentality, the new prospects in all fields of activity, and when one enters the Synagogue in Arhipova Street and sees the same old stereotypes, the 'establishment', the same indolence, the same fearful faces, one simply cannot find any explanation.

There are great possibilities of bringing about – if not with the official approval of the authorities, then with their tacit consent – the creation of a beginning of Jewish cultural and religious life, of organising communities at least in the big cities in each of which hundreds of thousands of Jews live.

Without wishing in the least to weaken our demand for Aliya, it must no longer hold the first or even the exclusive place on the agenda of the problem of Soviet Jews. What is a real drama is the situation of the millions who stay, who disappear, who literally disappear from the ranks of the Jewish people.

. . . One Sabbath, at the beginning of May 1975, I was at the Moscow Temple and, towards the end of the prayer, there appeared five or six persons who grouped themselves at the entrance. It was a group of 'refuseniks'. A Jew I had met as early as 1955, on my first visit to Moscow, came towards me. He was an engineer, strictly religious, who succeeded in observing the Sabbath. He asked me:

'Do you know Elie Wiesel? He launched the notion of "silent Jews". Are these people "silent Jews"? On the contrary. They are those who shout. But we, we who do not leave, who cannot leave, who wait for our children to leave, or even those who do not want to leave, are we not Jews? Does nobody speak for us? Is no voice raised so that we may remain Jews? Are we no longer Jews if we do not leave? And what about those who go to America or Australia? Are they better Jews than we are?' . . .

Our friends in England who are publishing this volume about their travels to the Jewish communities in Eastern Europe insisted on my writing this epilogue because they were expecting me to divulge in it . . . the recipe, i.e. to explain what I have done, what means I had resorted to so that the Jewish problem in Romania should be solved in four decades.

A recipe is something difficult. It is not only a matter of the components that have to be mixed up, but also of the way in which they are to be dosed. How much? How? When? are questions that are not easy to answer. What I have been trying to do in the above lines is just to give a retrospect of the problems, a new point of view and certain suggestions drawn from my own experience.

As God has helped me to survive this experience which, at a certain moment, in the years of Stalinism, could have proved fatal to me; as the miracle has occurred and I am able to give . . . consultations today concerning the recipes I used, then I am not allowed to refuse the nice travellers who came from beyond the Sambation.

Pour la bonne bouche, in conclusion, I would like to tell a joke.

A Jew had settled down in a railway carriage and, at the first station, he went to the window, looked out and made a gesture of surprise. Then he sat down once more. The train started again. At the next stop, our man went to the window, glanced out and . . . clutched at his head. The scene was repeated at the third station and our Jew seemed to be absolutely desperate.

The other passengers looked very puzzled at what was happening. Finally, the mystery was cleared up. The train was going in the opposite direction from the Jew's destination. Things got worse at every stop, for he was getting farther and farther away from his goal. Hence his growing despair.

'What am I to do?' he asked.

'That's quite simple. You must get off and take the train which is coming from the opposite direction. If you don't, it's no use clutching at your head and lamenting.'

Perhaps this joke can serve as . . . a recipe.

Publisher's note: This piece was written in 1987. In view of the recent changes in Eastern Europe we asked the author whether he had something to add, and his reply was, 'I maintain everything I wrote in 1987, but let me add, for clarification, the following':

These thoughts reflect the visit and the situation in 1987. But now, a new miracle has occurred in Jewish life – the opening of the gates of the Soviet Union. The excuse can now no longer be made that Soviet Jewry cannot be saved because of the terror in Russia. Soviet Jews now have the choice: to affirm their identity as Jews, or not. And if they affirm their identity as Jews, they also have the further choice: to go on Aliya, either now or later.

But there is a cost for this Aliya. In 1990 alone some 100,000 or more Jews will emigrate from the Soviet Union to Israel, and it will cost something like one billion dollars to provide even the basic resettlement requirements. The creation of employment will cost even more.

However, we must not under any circumstances forget the two million or so Soviet Jews who will choose to stay, or who may be unable to leave. As they represent mainly the fourth generation of Soviet Jews, they are all on the brink of disappearing into the anonymity of assimilation.

We need now to declare a Jewish glasnost, to recognise the reality of the Revolution which has taken place, with the consequent radical change in Jewish life. There are three million Jews in Russia and Eastern Europe, and they rely not only on other Jews but also on people throughout the world to arrange Aliya now, or to help maintain the Jewish communities by providing them with a Jewish infrastructure, with education and with religious teaching.

Nobody can know what may happen in the next few years. We have an unparalleled opportunity now to bring the Jews home to Israel. This opportunity may prove to be short-lived, so it must be taken. An enormous amount of money will be required immediately, both to resettle the Jews in Israel and also to provide the Jewish infrastructure for those who remain, since this is now permitted by the Soviet Government.

This is the challenge that now faces world Jewry, the miracle, the unbelievable opportunity to save the Jews of Eastern Europe. It can happen. It depends on us, and only on us – and, 'If we want, it will not be a legend.' It will be a reality.

Suggestions for further reading

Randolph Braham, *The Politics of Genocide: The Holocaust in Hungary*, 2 vols. (New York, 1981)

Lucy S. Dawidowicz, *The War Against the Jews* (New York and London, 1975–1985)

Celia Heller, *On the Edge of Destruction: Jews of Poland between the Two World Wars* (New York, 1977)

The Jews of Czechoslovakia, 3 vols. (Philadelphia, 1968, 1971 and 1983)

Paul Lendvai, *Antisemitism without Jews: Communist Eastern Europe* (London and New York, 1971)

William McCagg, *Jewish Nobles and Geniuses in Modern Hungary* (Boulder, 1972)

Ezra Mendelsohn, *The Jews of East Central Europe between the World Wars* (Bloomington: Indiana University Press, 1983)

Bela Vago, *The Shadow of the Swastika: The Rise of Fascism and Anti-Semitism in the Danube Basin 1936–1939* (London, 1975)

Bela Vago and George Mosse, eds., *Jews and Non-Jews in Eastern Europe, 1918–1945* (New York, 1974)

Jewish Identity Group

The Jewish Identity Group was established in 1978 with a view to studying the roots of Judaism and the development of various Jewish communities firstly in Eastern Europe but subsequently in India, Morocco, Turkey and other European countries.

In each case a short series of briefings was arranged by prominent speakers about the historical aspects of Jewish life in the countries concerned from the first known dates of Jewish settlement until the present day. The Group has been fortunate to find to-date the necessary expert local knowledge to assist in these briefings.

The highlight of each course was a visit to the country and community concerned to obtain first-hand knowledge and a greater understanding of what Jewish life is like today and to learn by speaking to the local community what they remember of life before the Holocaust. In each case every effort was made to have as a guide and scholar in residence for these visits, someone familiar with the country and who spoke the language, in addition to local representatives of the community itself.

Since its formation the Group has expanded considerably and interest has grown substantially. As a result of the historic changes that have taken place over the last few years, a recent visit was made to the Soviet Union and further visits are planned to certain Eastern European countries such as Poland and Czechoslovakia to study the current situation of the Jewish communities in the new political environment as compared to previous visits which were made several years ago under totally different circumstances. Only in this way is it possible to comprehend and appreciate the ever-changing situation of these small and remote communities and in some cases the difficult circumstances under which they manage to maintain and, sometimes, increase their Jewish identity.